Essential Topics in
MODERN BRITISH
POLITICS
and
GOVERNMENT

Phil Cocker and Alistair Jones

Liverpool Academic Press

© Phil Cocker and Alistair Jones 2005

Second edition published by Liverpool Academic Press, The Studio, High Green, Gt. Shelford, Cambridge CB2 5EG.

First edition published in Great Britain by Tudor Business Publishing Ltd.

ISBN 1 90349932 1

Typeset by Bitter & Twisted, bitter@cybase.co.uk
Graphics by K. Doughty

Printed in the UK by 4edge Limited - www.4edge.co.uk

CONTENTS

TABLES

ACKNOWLEDGEMENTS

There are a number of people who must be thanked for the support during the writing of this book. Top of the list is my wife, Claire, who has been helpful and supportive while I've been writing. Thanks must also go to Clive Gray, for his comments on so many of the chapters, and to Claire Drucquer (congratulations on the great 'A' level grades) who contributed a number of good ideas to the structure of the book. I must also thank all of my colleagues in the Department of Public Policy at De Montfort University for their support while I've been writing, as well as some of my students – most notably Richard Treffler. At home, our pets (Nua, Sasha and Hazel), as ever, need to be thanked for providing numerous distractions with their demands for feeding, walking or attention.

I would also like to thank Neil Fuller and David Barnes at Liverpool Academic Press and especially Phil Cocker, the original author, for giving me the opportunity to write this book.

Finally, as ever, if there are any mistakes or inaccuracies, the blame is mine. I hope that all of you who read this book get as much enjoyment out of it as I did in writing it.

Alistair Jones

CHAPTER ONE

Introduction – Britain, Politics and the Liberal Democratic State

INTRODUCTION

Politics is a subject that pervades every issue. It does not matter what issue is being discussed, it can be seen as having a political element to it. Despite this, the subject of politics seems to receive very bad press. It is boring, or not relevant, or – worst of all – it does not affect me. Much of this may be to do with the way in which politicians are presented in the media. Noting that bad news makes news, any indiscretion by a politician, at any level of government, is reported. Conversely, most of the good works of politicians go unreported.

Yet all of this is 'high' politics. The subjects of Parliament, local government, the European Union, the war in Iraq, they are all high politics. 'Low' politics, on the other hand, is to do with every day life. It could be a dispute in a school, a debate over redesigning a golf course, or neighbours discussing the trimming of a shared hedge. All of these examples contain politics. It is there in our television programmes – even the soap operas.

Politics

Although there is no agreed definition of politics among political scientists, there are a number of key features that exist through many definitions. Politics is about conflict and conflict resolution. This can be over the ownership and distribution of resources. It is also about government and finding appropriate acceptable solutions to problems. Politics need not contain violence, although much of the language used presents such a connotation.

What is Politics?

So, what is politics? Politics is about conflict and conflict resolution. It is also about control. In fact, politics can be portrayed as a continual loop: control – conflict – conflict resolution – control – conflict, etc. But the control of, or conflict over, what? The answer is anything. To present a hypothetical example: two households are separated by a hedge. One of these 'owns' the hedge, and is responsible for its maintenance. The owner of the hedge refuses to cut it, and it grows ever higher, blocking out the sunlight in the neighbouring garden. Thus the owner of the hedge has control. The neighbour asks that the hedge be cut. This is the conflict. The owner can agree and cut the hedge. In doing so, the conflict is resolved, although the control remains the same. If the owner refuses to cut the hedge, the conflict will continue with the neighbour searching for alternative means in which to get the hedge cut. A mediator could be called in, such as the local council or the Citizen's Advice Bureau, in an effort to resolve the conflict. Conflict resolution will only occur when both parties agree to a solution, or if a solution is imposed upon them by an outside body. In this particular circumstance, the council could intervene and have the hedge cut.

The title of Harold Lasswells text sums up what Politics is all about: Politics: Who Gets What, When, How (McGraw-Hill, 1936). At the national and international level, it can be seen as a fight for scarce resources and their subsequent redistribution - and with the consumption rates in today's world, these resources are getting scarcer. At the local level, it is no different. The disputes may be on a smaller scale but they are still over scarce resources.

Liberal democracy

In Britain, we live in a liberal democracy. A democracy is about people ruling. The term comes from the Greek: demos (the people) and kratos (rule or power). Hence, rule of the people. In theory at least, everyone has a role to play in a democracy. A liberal democracy means that we have rights, duties and obligations as well. There are a number of features that characterise a liberal democracy, and these are listed in Table 1.1. In theory, all of these characteristics exist in a liberal democracy, and ought to be protected – working on the premise that liberal democracy is a valid system for ruling to begin with.

Looking at the list of features in Table 1.1, the first thing to note is that there are flaws in most items. We have a secret ballot, but all of the ballot papers are numbered. To be able to vote, you must be on the electoral register. A prominent supporter of electoral reform is Prince Charles, but he does not have the right to vote. Representative government sounds impressive, but representative of whom? Is it the people, or the party in power, or even the financial backers and sponsors? As for the free press, there have been instances of the government blocking publication of news through the use of Defence Notices. Finally, there are our basic liberal freedoms. This subject will be examined in Chapter Four, but it is important to note here that these freedoms can be suspended at any time by the government.

Table 1.1 Features of a liberal democracy

- ❏ Regular free elections
- ❏ Secret ballot
- ❏ The right to vote for all adults
- ❏ Representative government
- ❏ Provision for Opposition parties to operate freely
- ❏ A free press
- ❏ The basic liberal freedoms including:
  - ❏ free speech
  - ❏ freedom of movement
  - ❏ freedom of association
  - ❏ freedom of religious expression

The State

Finally, there is the State. This term carries many negative connotations, just like the concept politics. In a similar fashion, these may be unjustified. Louis XIV of France decreed «L'etat c'est moi» (I am the State). He was a symbol of the divine power of monarchs.

The modern state can be presented in a number of ways, and not all of them are necessarily compatible with the concept of liberal democracy (see Table 1.2). In the most general of terms, a state has clearly defined geographical boundaries and is the supreme law making body within those boundaries. As such, it is able to control the population. It is sovereign. There will be a political apparatus to rule over the territory, with such features as a Parliament, a legal system and a bureaucracy. There will also be an army to protect the State from external interference. Within the State there will be some form of policing to maintain law and order.

A State also confers legitimacy. This can be external in that other states recognize the right of a state to govern within its geographical boundaries. It can also be internal, where the State has, for example, a monopoly of 'legitimate violence' – the ability to ensure the obedience of the people, by punishing those who break the law. Internal legitimately, at its most basic level, means that the public accepts that the State has the right to govern.

Table 1.2 Components of the State

- ❏ Sovereign territory
- ❏ Centralised authority
- ❏ Funded through taxation
- ❏ Bureaucracy
- ❏ Allegiance/loyalty
- ❏ Representative government
- ❏ Citizenship
- ❏ Nationalism

The State is a sizeable body, with many component parts. As will be seen in Chapter Sixteen, it can be presented as an overbearing body that needs to be reined in and reduced in size. What cannot be disputed is the need for a State, even if it is only within a co-ordinating role. Arguably, the way in which the European Union is developing is towards what has been described as a "super-State". The language used in some parts of the media presents such a move as being undesirable, as it undermines the role of the State – suggesting that a State is needed. The particular functions that are carried out by the State still need to be carried out. This merely emphasises the importance of the role of the State, while also highlighting how the State can evolve and how states may merge to enhance their own well being.

Content of the book

This book is a compilation of a series of short essays. The object is to select key areas in the curriculum, and then select specific questions to address within each area. Thus each chapter contains an introduction, where any key concepts are defined. Thereafter, a topical questioned is addressed, with both sides of the question being examined. Each chapter concludes with a summary of key points.

The objective in this book is to highlight that there are at least two perspectives that can be used when addressing any question. When answering essays or exam questions it is imperative that this be borne in mind. Too often, students simply address only one aspect of a question, even when asked to "discuss" or "comment" on a particular issue. An answer does not have to be totally even handed. It is important to note that there will always be counter-arguments that can be presented.

Each chapter in this book presents two sides to a particular question or topic. What must be noted is that these are only perspectives on the subject. They are not categoric answers. Politics is not that clear cut. Thus each perspective can be refuted.

The following chapters focus on a number of key topics, from Parliament and central government, to voting, devolution and the EU. The concluding chapter will pull the disparate strands of the book together. Each chapter may be read in isolation but there are links running across a range of them for cross-referencing purposes. Enthusiasts may wish to read the book from cover to cover, and I would dissuade no one from doing that. Similarly, for those who wish to cherry pick for particular essays or exam revision, only individual chapters will be relevant. There is no harm in this, but I would advise being prepared to read a little more widely via the cross-referencing links. At the end of each chapter is a summary of key points (as can be seen below). There are also other references and internet sites which may be of use.

Summary of key points

WHAT IS POLITICS?

- No agreed definition
- It is about conflict, conflict resolution and control
- Politics is about competition for scarce resources
- It is also about the role of government

LIBERAL DEMOCRACY

- Democracy is about people ruling
- A liberal democracy emphasizes electoral processes to select the government of the day
- The basic liberal freedoms should be protected (e.g. freedom of speech, of movement, of association, etc.)

THE STATE

- Clearly defined geographical boundaries within which the State is sovereign
- There are legislative and judicial bodies
- It is administered by a bureaucracy
- In the modern State, there is representative government – democracy

Further Reading

Cocker, P. and Jones, A.; *Contemporary British Politics and Government* (Liverpool Academic Press, 2002) 2nd edition

Lasswell, H.; *Politics: Who Gets What, When, How* (McGraw-Hill, 1936)

Orwell, G.; *1984* (Penguin, 1990)

Internet sources

www.psa.ac.uk

This is the home page of the British Political Studies Association

www.psr.keele.ac.uk/

Richard Kimber's Political Science Resources. From here you can access almost any topic in British Politics, or even international subjects.

CHAPTER TWO

Political Culture

INTRODUCTION

The concept of political culture is rather difficult to define. It is often confused with the actions of people, whereas it is actually to do with thoughts. In fact our actions and thoughts are not always similar.

Political culture is to do with peoples' thoughts, beliefs, knowledge and attitudes about politics, government, and society. It involves the collective attitudes of the entire population rather than that of an individual. Thus a stereotypical image of the British political culture might emphasize a homogeneous society; a general consensus over the conduct of politics; deference towards both members and institutions of state; and, civility in the way in which political disputes are resolved. Almond and Verba's *The Civic Culture* (1963) highlighted these types of ideas in their analysis of the British political culture. While such a perspective is no longer considered accurate (assuming it ever was), it is still seen as the image of the British – a stiff upper lip in the face of adversity; an unwillingness to 'rock the boat' or cause trouble.

> **Political Culture**
>
> This is to do with peoples' thoughts, values, knowledge and beliefs about politics, government and society. It acknowledges that thoughts and perceptions are as important as actions – and in fact that peoples thoughts and actions may differ.

Political culture is passed on through socialization. This is, in effect, the way an individual acquires an understanding of politics and also his/her place in politics. Socialisation is traditionally viewed as being carried out through the family, with parents, or any relatives, communicating ideas, thoughts, etc. to children. However, more recently, the role of the media has been highlighted, with political ideas and values being transmitted to all viewers/readers/listeners. A more radical perspective is that the media actually carries out some form of indoctrination.

There are three strands to political culture. Firstly, there is cognition. This is to do with knowledge. Specifically, it is knowledge of such things as one's country or political system. Secondly, there is affection, which links feelings to the knowledge. How much pride do you feel for your country or your leader? Finally there is evaluation. This focuses upon the judgments that people may make about both their knowledge and their feelings – in effect, are the leaders doing a good job running the country. If there is no cognition, there can be no affection or evaluation.

Political culture is therefore to do with peoples' thoughts and perceptions about a range of areas. These can include politics, government, and even self-perception – for example, the perception of nationality.

Are We All British?

The case for everyone being British

A key aspect of why we are all British is the history of these islands. What is interesting about the history of Britain is the lack of radical change since the Norman invasion in 1066. While there has been the War of the Roses (1455-87), the Civil War and the Interregnum (1640-60), the Glorious Revolution of 1688, and the Acts of Union of 1707 and 1801, these periods of change have been absorbed into an apparently seamless history. Many of the symbols and ceremonies that are still in existence today can be dated back to medieval times or even earlier. They have evolved over time, along with the procedures of Government. The revolutions that have occurred in Britain have not been as fundamental as those of, for example, France or the USA. The so-called revolutions in Britain have been little more than spats between sections of the ruling classes.

What has been emphasised in the history of Britain is consensus. Even when there have been severe disagreements between the various sections of the ruling classes, these have been resolved and a new consensus reached. It has also meant that when there have been external challenges the British have been able to present a united front to the enemy.

Closely linked to the historical evolution of Britain has been a high degree of stability. As noted above, there has been a gradual process of change. For the most part, there have been no violent upheavals (except in Northern Ireland). There is an apparent consensus, with the majority of the population being reasonably happy with the way in which the country is run. There is a balance between effective government and a right to opposition. On occasions, popular protest may arise as a consequence of particular policies. But there tends not to be a demand to overthrow the government *per se* (just the specific post holders). Even the General Strike of 1926 did not make such demands.

However, a footnote is required here. This picture of a stable country that has evolved over time is something of an idealised portrait – and one that is encouraged in some sections of the British media. There are sections of British history which are glossed over, such as the Tolpuddle martyrs, the Chartists, the Jarrow marchers, the suffragettes (and their treatment by the State), Scottish rebellions, or, more recently, central government operations in Northern Ireland. To this list we can also add the treatment of immigrants and asylum seekers. When such concerns are raised, accusations suddenly fly of people trying to rewrite history for their own purposes. The sanitised idyll is considered by some to be far more preferable than the rather messy reality.

Part of the explanation of the stability of the United Kingdom has been the innate conservatism of the British public with deferential attitudes to authority, to class 'superiors', to obedience to the law. This is manifest in reverence for institutions like the monarchy. High levels of support for the monarchy were found during the Golden Jubilee celebrations in 2002. Added to this, there are also inclinations to regard the monarchy and the aristocracy as socially superior. Caricatures can be conjured up of cap-doffing workers who know their place and desire that those who have been reared and educated to govern should do so. There is a grain of truth in this caricature – in fact maybe more so when looking at the support for issues such as fox hunting.

Deference has also been ascribed to some voting patterns. This is often highlighted when examining working class electoral support for the Conservative Party. The Conservatives are usually portrayed as the middle class party, many of whose members are the social superiors who have been reared and educated to rule. Traditional working class Tories may perceive the Labour Party as little more than a group of upstarts who are trying to destroy the traditional way of running the country. While this may be something of an oversimplification, the Conservative Party has been viewed as the party which represents tradition and continuity. Deferential support from the working classes simply entrenches this perspective.

A final aspect of why we may all be viewed as British is social homogeneity. This focuses upon the social composition and attitudes of the British. Although there are pronounced class differences that could be a source of disharmony, in Britain class almost acts as cement binding the nation in a recognised system. This class system is not rigid, as there are opportunities for individuals to climb the ladder of success. In 1967, Pulzer claimed that class was "the basis of British party politics; all else is embellishment and detail". While such a claim may no longer be quite so valid today, class is still an important factor.

Even from an ethnic minority perspective, there now appears to be a general feeling of being 'British'. A survey from the Office of National

Statistics (in January 2004) found that a majority of Black and Asian people in Britain saw themselves as being 'British' (see *www.statistics.gov.uk/CCI/ nugget.asp?ID=459&Pos1&ColRank=2&Rank=1000* for more information).

The idea of being British does not simply apply to people who are born in this country, but also to many who now reside here.

However, the social homogeneity factor should not be overstated. Beneath the veneer of social stability there are a range of tensions. Some of these became apparent during the rioting in 2001 in the North of England. These served as a reminder that the fabric of society might not be as strong as many would like it to be.

The case against everyone being British

The United Kingdom is made up of distinct parts, most notably Scotland, England, Northern Ireland and Wales. Each of these has specific national characteristics, as evidenced in the language, religion, history and culture. These are the objective features of nationalism. Added to this there are also the subjective features of nationalism - particularly the awareness of, and feeling for, ones' nationality.

This nationalism is strengthened through adversity. There appears to be an almost global mindset that being 'British' is the same as 'English'. It does not matter if you come from Kelvinside or Llanelli, there appears to be an assumption that you are English. The reaction is an adamant anti-English one which highlights and strengthens ones' own nationality. It is as bad as describing a Canadian as being an American, or a New Zealander as an Australian. Nationalism is a strong challenge to the idea of a British political culture. Such a concern was highlighted in the Commission on the Future of Multi-Ethnic Britain (October 2000):

> Many customary images of Britain are English-centred - and, indeed, southern English-centred - and leaving many millions out of the picture. Increasingly in Scotland and Wales people have a sense of multiple identity. Also, Englishness is in the process of being redefined. (*www.runnymedetrust.org/meb/TheReport.htm*)

An example of the problem of images being English-centred could be seen when Michael Douglas, in his role as United Nations Ambassador for Nuclear Disarmament, spoke to MPs in March 2000 on the Non-proliferation Treaty. Douglas pointed out that 'England' was one of the five nuclear powers, and that 'England' was uniquely placed to solve problems between the USA and Russia. His speech was later sanitised by some branches of the media, with references being made to the UK and Britain, rather than England.

This lack of knowledge may be portrayed as harmless ignorance in some quarters (particularly in England), even when the guilty party has a Welsh wife. Yet to the non-English nationalities in Britain, the supposition that the terms 'English' and 'British' are tantamount to the same thing is particularly hurtful. It glosses over regional and ethnic disparities, and the English-based media appear willing to collude in such actions. It sometimes results in a virulent anti-English backlash. The reporting of success of 'British' sportspeople is particularly interesting. Ian Woosnam is a 'British' golfer when he wins a tournament, but is 'Welsh' when he loses. For Colin Montgomerie, replace Welsh with Scottish. Conversely, English sportspeople are English when they win but British when they lose.

This challenge to being British has further manifested itself in some political activities, where actions have strengthened thoughts. The devolution legislation of the late 1990s, which created a Scottish Parliament and assemblies in Northern Ireland and Wales, has provided a national focal point where nationalist thoughts can be directed. The importance of these directly elected bodies is such that they are now considered as being more important than the British Parliament by some members of the general public in Scotland and Wales. Thus these bodies have increased feelings of nationalism and separateness from Britain. Arguably, as foreseen by Tam Dalyell, devolution could lead to the break up of the United Kingdom.

In 2001, the National Centre for Social Research found that fewer people in Britain than ever before identified themselves as 'British'. Eighty per cent of Scots identified themselves as 'Scottish', and only 13% as 'British'. The English were more likely to describe themselves as 'British', with 47% doing so. However 41% of those surveyed described themselves as 'English' (*www.natcen.ac.uk/news/news_bsa_pr2001.htm*). It seems that the 'British' national identity is being eroded away.

Yet it is not just nationalism that undermines the idea of being British, but also ethnic diversity. The divisions that exist within Britain are not just to do with the indigenous nationalities. Britain is a multi-cultural society. Approximately 5.5% of the British population is comprised of ethnic minorities. There is much evidence to support accusations of discrimination against ethnic minorities. In fact, the Macpherson Report into the Stephen Lawrence murder case accused the Metropolitan Police not only of racism, but institutional racism.

> Para. 6.4 "Racism" in general terms consists of conduct or words
> or practices which advantage or disadvantage people because of
> their colour, culture or ethnic origin. In its more subtle form it
> is as damaging as in its overt form.

> Para 6.34 "Institutional racism" consists of the collective
> failure of an organisation to provide an appropriate and
> professional service to people because or their colour, culture
> or ethnic origin. It can be seen or detected in processes,
> attitudes and behaviour which amount to discrimination
> through unwitting prejudice, ignorance, thoughtlessness, and
> racist stereotyping which disadvantage minority people.

The racial discrimination that exists has caused huge problems. There have
been sporadic race riots in England since the late 1950s. The most recent of
these occurred during the 2001 General Election campaign in Oldham and
other towns in the North of England.

In the 1980s, Norman Tebbitt (now Lord Tebbitt) suggested some form of
citizenship test for all immigrants to Britain. The Tebbitt test, as it was labelled,
proposed asking any new immigrant which cricket team they supported – the
expectation being that the response would be Britain (or more accurately in
the case of cricket, England). The idea was, supposedly, to instil some feeling
of being 'British'. Looking at the exuberance displayed when England lose at
cricket to Pakistan (or India, Sri Lanka, the West Indies, Australia, New Zealand
or South Africa), it seems that more and more people are failing the Tebbitt
test.

The European Union has also had an impact upon Britain. Since joining
what was the EEC in 1973, Britain has become drawn into Europe. People in
Britain no longer hold British passports, but rather EU passports. There are
supposedly no internal frontiers within the EU, meaning that people should be
able to travel anywhere without needing their passports. The growth and
influence of the EU has been phenomenal. There has been the replacement
of most imperial weights and measures with metric counterparts; there is the
possible introduction of the Euro; there are common policies in areas such as
agriculture, fisheries, and competition – all of these show the extent to which
Britain is becoming 'Europeanised'. In fact, Ben Rosamund has written about
"The Europeanization of British Politics".

Margaret Thatcher, in 1988, complained that the people of Europe could
become 'identikit Europeans'. In a speech to the College of Europe in Bruges,
she said:

> My first guiding principle is this: willing and active co-operation
> between independent sovereign states... Europe will be stronger
> precisely because it has France as France, Spain as Spain, Britain
> as Britain, each with its own customs, traditions and identity. It

would be folly to try to fit them into some sort of identikit
European personality.

(*www.margaretthatcher.com*)

Although Thatcher was considered to have been rather extreme in her
outlook, she did raise a spectre that has caused much concern in Britain. To
some degree, such a concern has not disappeared over time. Rather, the
tabloid press has played upon the fears of the British people becoming
'Europeans', and have presented such a scenario in a very negative light.
However, it is possible to be both British and European, or even Scottish,
British and European – although from an independent Scotland perspective, it
is possible to be both Scottish and European, but not necessarily British.

Conclusion

When looking at political culture, and asking if we are all British, the answer
is not as clear cut as some would like. There is no definitive answer. The cases,
both for and against, are credible. The problem is the complicated issue of
nationality. Individual perceptions of 'nationality' are not always clear.
Norman Tebbitt has argued that you cannot belong to two nations – in this
case, he may be wrong. What decides a persons' nationality? Is their place
of birth, or the nationality of their parents? Of course, if it is the latter, how
was their nationality determined? To present a hypothetical example: if some
one is born in Gibraltar, is this person Gibraltarian or British? If Gibraltar is
ceded to Spain, does everyone living there become Spanish? Nationality is
extremely complex.

Added to this, when examining if we are all British, there are the overseas
perceptions of the British. Not only is there the example of the confusion
between England and Britain, as demonstrated by Michael Douglas (cited
earlier in this chapter), but we can also look to opinion poll/survey data. A
special report in the *Guardian* in November 2000 was headlined "World's
youth see Britons as racist drunks". Surveys of young people from around the
world found that the British were seen as arrogant, condescending and always
drunk. Such perceptions were created, or more likely enhanced, by some
British (or English) football supporters abroad. In nation-specific questions,
Scotland was associated with kilts and whisky; Northern Ireland with violence
and religious war; Wales with Diana, Princess of Wales and the Prince of Wales;
and England with the Queen and the Royal Family, and London. The best-
known Britons were Tony Blair and the Spice Girls. Overseas perceptions of
Britain appear rather peculiar. Among the European countries surveyed,

Britain was most popular with France!

The problem, if it is perceived as such, is how to counteract some of these negative images. The government has set up a task force to find ways to improve Britain's image overseas. It is going to be a long slow process, and it is one which is based on the assumption that we are all British.

Summary of key points

DEFINITION OF POLITICAL CULTURE

❑   It is about thoughts, beliefs, knowledge and attitudes about politics, government, society, etc

❑   It is passed on through socialisation

THE CASE FOR EVERYONE BEING BRITISH

❑   Evolution of the 'British' State

❑   Stability within Britain

❑   Deference

❑   Social homogeneity

THE CASE AGAINST EVERYONE BEING BRITISH

❑   Nationalism – Scottish, English, Irish and Welsh

❑   Ethnic diversity

❑   Development of Europe

Further Reading

Almond, G. and Verba, S.; *The Civic Culture* (Princeton University Press, 1963)

Almond, G. and Verba, S.; *The Civic Culture Revisited* (Little, Brown and Company, 1980)

Dell'Olio, F.; "The Redefinition of the Concept of Nationality in the UK" *Politics* vol. 22 (2002)

Gamble, A.; *Between Europe and America: The Future of British Politics* (Palgrave, 2003)

Jessop, B.; *Traditional Conservatism and British Political Culture* (George, Allen and Unwin, 1974)

Kavanagh, D.; *Political Culture* (Macmillan, 1972)

Rosamund, B.; "The Europeanization of British Politics" in Dunleavy, P., Gamble, A., Heffernan, R. and Peele, G. (eds.); *Developments in British Politics 7* (Palgrave, 2003)

Internet Sites

www.guardian.co.uk

The Guardian archive has a number of stories on political culture and national identity in Britain

www.official-documents.co.uk/document/cm42/4262/4262.htm

The official report of the Stephen Lawrence Inquiry, headed by Sir William Macpherson of Cluny

www.runnymedetrust.org/meb/TheReport.htm

This is the report of the Commission on the Future of Multi-Ethnic Britain. From here it is also possible to access reports on the report

www.statistics.gov.uk/CCI/nugget.asp?ID=459&Pos1&ColRank=2&Rank=1000

The Office of National Statistics Report on being British

CHAPTER THREE

The Constitution

INTRODUCTION

Constitutions are often presented as great documents that detail the role of government; weighty tomes that only lawyers and judges can understand. The perception of a constitution is of a dusty document, that the average person has no hope whatsoever of understanding. The British constitution is not like this. In fact, it could actually be viewed as being worse!

A constitution may be viewed as the 'rules of the political game'. In the same way that different sports have their rules and regulations, the way in which politics operates is governed by the constitution. There are many different types of constitution. One type of categorisation is between federal and unitary constitutions. A federal constitution disperses power to different parts of the country e.g. the USA and Germany. Different tiers of government are allocated different powers and responsibilities, and these are protected by the constitution. Britain, on the other hand, has a unitary constitution. This means that legislative power is centralised to a single source – in Britain's case: Parliament. The United Kingdom (England, Scotland, Northern Ireland and Wales) is governed by Parliament. Devolution has some effect on Britain's unitary constitution. While there may be two legislative bodies in Scotland, Northern Ireland and Wales, they are secondary to the Westminster Parliament. Legislative power may be handed down from Westminster but such power may be withdrawn by Westminster.

Constitution

This is the 'rule book' as to how politics may operate in a country. A constitution allocates powers and responsibilities to different bodies and post-holders. A constitution may be written or unwritten, codified or uncodified.

Other types of categorisation of constitutions are written or unwritten, and codified or uncodified. As the label suggests, a written constitution is written down while an unwritten constitution is not. A codified constitution is encompassed in a single document, as in the case of the USA. An uncodified constitution may be written down but it is not contained in a single document. The British constitution is often described as being unwritten, but this is inaccurate. The British constitution is partially written but uncodified. Some parts of the British constitution are written down, others are not. This makes it difficult to find all the different parts of the British constitution. It means that people may not know the actual rules of the political game. For ease, they are detailed in Table 3.1. The problem is that if people do not know the rules, should they not be written down for ease of access?

Table 3.1 Components of the British Constitution

Component	Explanation	Example
Statute law	Acts of Parliament which override other constitutional sources	Parliament Act 1911 Parliament Act 1949 European Communities Act 1972
Common law	Judicial decisions which establish legal precedents	Freedom of speech, movement, association, etc.
Conventions	Rules, customs and practices which are considered binding (normally applicable to Parliament)	Collective responsibility of the Cabinet Prime Minister is a member of the House of Commons
EU law	This takes precedence over national law (where the two conflict)	Treaty of European Union 1992 Treaty of Nice 2000
Law and custom of Parliament	Guidelines as to how Parliament may operate	Impartiality of Parliament the Speaker. The guidelines are detailed in Erskine May (1844); *Treatise on the Law, Privileges, Proceedings, and Usage of Parliament*
Works of authority	Books and writings which are considered as expert guidance on the constitution	W. Bagehot (1867); *The English Constitution* A.V. Dicey (1885); *An Introduction to the Study of the Law of the Constitution*

Does Britain need a written Constitution?

The case against a written constitution

As noted above, the British constitution is already partially written. Those opposed to any change highlight the great flexibility in having such a constitution. It is adaptable and can easily respond to change. This can be compared to the US constitution which is written and codified, and extremely difficult to change. In over two centuries, there have only been 27 amendments to the US constitution, and ten of these were the original Bill of Rights which was adopted in 1791. The twenty seventh amendment was ratified in 1992, on the compensation for services of elected politicians. Some of the amendments have also been reversed e.g. the eighteenth amendment which introduced prohibition was repealed by the twenty first amendment. This effectively means that the USA of the twenty first century is still running under the rigid guidelines of a document which is well over two hundred years old. The world has changed markedly since US independence but the US constitution has hardly changed at all. Conversely, the British constitution has gradually evolved over the same period of time, although at a somewhat greater speed in more recent years. Examples of the gradual change include the balance of power changing between the two Houses of Parliament; the role of the Monarch in relation to Parliament and the paying of taxes; voting rights; joining the EEC; and the proposed abolition of the post of Lord Chancellor (to be replaced by a Department of Constitutional Affairs) and introduction of some form of Supreme Court.

The key feature of the British constitution is Parliamentary sovereignty. This means that Parliament is the supreme law making body in Britain. Laws are made by elected representatives rather than by appointed judges. Since Parliament derives its legitimacy and its strength from the consent of the governed, and is accountable to the voters, it is considered that adequate checks and balances exist to prevent the emergence of an autocratic executive. A strong executive is encouraged, as noted by Bagehot in 1867, but it is always accountable to Parliament.

A.V. Dicey wrote in 1885 that Parliamentary sovereignty was

> The right to make or unmake any law whatever; and... that no person or body is recognised by the law of England as having a right to override or set aside the legislation of Parliament. (1959, pp. 39–40)

Parliament is not only the supreme law making body, but any decisions or laws made by Parliament may only be reversed or repealed by Parliament. Basically, Parliament may not bind its' successors. This convention is also an example of how well the constitution works at the moment.

The flexibility of the British constitution has been demonstrated very clearly over the last few years. The Blair Government has introduced a number of constitutional reforms, often under the guise of "modernisation": for example devolution, reform of the House of Lords, the introduction of proportional representation for elections to the European Parliament and to new bodies such as the Welsh Assembly and the Greater London Authority, signing up to the Social Charter (as part of the Treaty of European Union of 1992) and to the Treaty of Amsterdam. Had the British constitution been fully written then these reforms might never have taken place (noting the difficulty in amending the US constitution). In fact the further development of the EU, with both widening and deepening of membership, may be viewed as continual constitutional change. It is important to note that this constitutional change can also be reversed by withdrawing from the EU. As Parliament cannot bind its' successors, a simple Act of Parliament would enable Britain to withdraw. Thus parts of the constitution would revert back to how they were prior to 1973.

The basic mentality behind opposition to a fully written constitution is the idea that "if it ain't broke, don't fix it". The British constitution is working. It is by no means perfect but it is evolving and developing to adjust to life in the twenty first century. The formal writing and presumable codification would hinder this adaptability. Added to this, who would 'write' the unwritten sections? The public does not exactly trust politicians, or lawyers, or judges. A constitution written by committee would probably end up trying to be all things to all people. It is far better to leave well alone.

The case in favour of a written constitution

For the most part, the arguments in favour of a fully written constitution for Britain are based on refuting the arguments against. The British constitution is not as flexible as many might argue. Parliament is dominated by the Executive to such a degree that it is very rare for Parliament to defeat government legislation. Thus a strong executive with a large majority in the House of Commons could railroad through any legislation that it wishes e.g. Blunkett after September 11. Another example is the current reform of the House of Lords. A large number of MPs, particularly Liberal Democrats and Conservatives but also some from the Labour benches, wish to see a fully elected second chamber. Tony Blair declared that a fully appointed second chamber would be far better. Thus he decided to ignore the recommendations of the Wakeham Commission which proposed a partially-elected body. Blair appeared likely to force this constitutional change through Parliament and there was nothing that could be done to stop him (although he did promise a 'free vote' on the issue). In fact all proposed options for a new second chamber were defeated. This left a largely appointed second chamber, with a handful of hereditary peers – which is almost exactly what Blair wanted! While it is possible to portray Blair's actions as a potential abuse of power, a fully written constitution could prevent such actions by, for example, only permitting such constitutional change with either a referendum or a two thirds majority in Parliament on a free vote. Thus the public would be guaranteed some form of consultation, either directly or indirectly. However, this is unlikely to happen with the constitution at the moment. A strong executive can force through any legislation it so wishes. In fact, the executive can even restructure itself without necessarily explaining the actions to Parliament. In the 2003 cabinet reshuffle, the post of Lord Chancellor and the Secretary of State for Scotland and for Wales were all abolished. Admittedly, the post of Lord Chancellor was replaced by a Secretary of State for Constitutional Affairs, but Scotland and Wales were reduced to having other ministers acting as spokespersons in the cabinet. In 1976, Lord Hailsham described such the situation of a strong executive as an "elective dictatorship" (*The Listener*, 21 October 1976). It seems that very little has changed.

To complicate matters still further, a subsequent government could reverse any of these decisions. Blair's proposed appointed second chamber could be abolished altogether, or replaced by a partially-elected or fully elected chamber. As no Parliament can bind its' successors, any of these constitutional changes could be reversed at any time. All of this could be changed with a fully written constitution – including the convention of Parliament not being able to bind its' successors.

The role of the European Union in Britain is written down. The various treaties that founded and developed the organisation (Paris (1951), Rome (1957), Treaty of Accession (1972), European Union (1992), Amsterdam (1997) and Nice (2000)) are all written down and enacted. They could of course all be repealed if Britain withdraws from the EU. However, while Britain is a member of the EU, European law takes precedence over British law should the two conflict. In theory, this position could be viewed as undermining Parliamentary sovereignty and thus the major premise on which the entire British constitution is based (although the option of withdrawal arguably counters this argument). However, it does mean that Europe can actually make decisions to which Britain must adhere.

However, with only a partially written constitution, in the future it may be possible for constitutional change to take place through EU intervention, without Britain being able to prevent such change. At the moment, constitutional change usually requires unanimity among all member states. Whereas this may be a case of the British Parliament passing the appropriate legislation, in the Republic of Ireland a referendum is required to accept any EU treaty that may cause constitutional change. Thus the Treaty of Nice (2000), which focused upon EU enlargement, was taken to a referendum in

Ireland. This referendum came out against the treaty. Thus it could not be ratified in Ireland and therefore could not be accepted as an EU treaty as all member states had to support the treaty. Ireland later held a second referendum which reversed the original decision.

A fully written constitution would present the opportunity for the inclusion of a complete Bill of Rights. While this specific question is actually addressed in Chapter Four, it is worthy of a brief mention here. Currently, Britain has a Human Rights Act which was passed in 1998 and came into effect in 2000. The legislation was based upon the European Convention on Human Rights. However, this legislation can be repealed by another Act of Parliament, and can even be suspended – as was the case in the aftermath of the terrorist attack on the World Trade Centre in New York. If the Human Rights Act (or a Bill of Rights) was to be included in a fully written constitution, as is the case in the USA, there would be a benchmark of rights with which no government would be able to tamper on a whim. At the same time it is important to note that such a document could be changed by constitutional amendment – as is the case in the USA.

A final point to note is that a fully written constitution could also present an opportunity to include a proper Freedom of Information Act. As with the case of the Human Rights Act, the current legislation on Freedom of Information could be reversed by another Act of Parliament. A protected right of access to official data and information could create a more open government and society than we have at the moment. The emphasis in government is still upon secrecy, with legislation such as the Official Secrets Act. The current Blair Government, like its predecessor claims to want Open Government. There would be a greater chance of achieving this with freedom of information legislation protected within a fully written constitution.

Conclusion

The issue of Britain adopting a fully written constitution is a complicated one. There are a number of factors, detailed throughout the chapter, which need to be taken into consideration. The primary one is whether or not Britain needs to change the current constitutional set up. The extensive changes to the constitution that have been enacted by the current Labour Government demonstrate that the flexibility of the British constitution remains. Many of the changes introduced by the Labour Government could be reversed by a successor, which highlights the flexibility of the current constitutional arrangements. However, it appears unlikely that the decisions will be repealed, as demonstrated with the current all-party support for policies such as devolution, but it is not impossible from a constitutional perspective. Added to this, there have been a number of proposed changes that have not taken place (e.g. electoral reform for Parliamentary elections), and others that have been fudged (e.g. reform of the House of Lords).

What we are currently seeing in mainstream political circles is a lack of debate over the British constitution. There is ambiguity in the British constitution, and it will be present as long as unwritten custom and convention remain as features of the constitution. By writing these aspects down in law, the ambiguities will not necessarily disappear. If anything, the ambiguities may simply become more legalistic.

What is interesting in Britain is that the general public, for the most part, appear unaware of the British constitution. This can be compared to countries such as the USA, where the opposite appears to be the case – at least in respect of the Bill of Rights. What is apparent is that the US constitution is a very important reference point for most Americans. It is underpinned by their education system, where pupils are made aware of the constitution and the Bill of Rights. Trying to teach British pupils about the constitution is far more difficult considering that parts of it are not written down.

Summary of key points

DEFINITION OF THE CONSTITUTION

❏ The 'rules of the political game'

❏ A constitution details how politics operates in a country

❏ A constitution may be 'written' or 'unwritten', 'codified' or 'uncodified'

❏ It allocates powers and responsibilities

THE CASE AGAINST A WRITTEN CONSTITUTION

❏ The UK constitution is already partially written

❏ A written constitution could transfer power from Parliament to the judiciary

❏ The flexibility of the current situation (which has served Britain well) would be lost

❏ The British constitution is able to evolve in its current format

THE CASE FOR A WRITTEN CONSTITUTION

❏ The flexibility argument is a myth

❏ Prime Ministerial dominance of Parliament

❏ "Elective Dictatorship"

Further Reading

Bagehot, W.; *The English Constitution* (originally 1867; Fontana/Collins, 1963 with Introduction by R. H. S. Crossman)

Dicey, A.V.; *An Introduction to the Study of the Law of the Constitution* (Macmillan, 1959) 10th edition. Originally published in 1885.

Hailsham, Lord; "Elective Dictatorship" *The Listener* 21 October 1976

Jowell, J. and Oliver, D. (eds.); *The Changing Constitution* (Oxford University Press, 2000, 4th ed.)

Madgwick, P. and Woodhouse, D.; *The Law and Politics of the Constitution of the United Kingdom* (Harvester Wheatsheaf, 1995)

Marshall, G.; *Constitutional Conventions: The Rules and Forms of Political Accountability* (Clarendon Press, 1984)

Pilkington, C.; "A constitutional question: the United Kingdom or federal Britain?" in Robins, L. and Jones, B. (eds.); *Debates in British Politics Today* (Manchester University Press, 2000.)

Internet sources

www.hmso.gov.uk/acts/acts2000/20000036.htm

Freedom of Information Act

www.ucl.ac.uk/constitution-unit

Homepage of the Constitution Unit at University College London. This website gives access to comprehensive overviews of the constitutional changes that have taken place since 1997

CHAPTER FOUR

Bill of Rights/Human Rights Act

INTRODUCTION

The debate over whether or not Britain needs a Bill of Rights (or more accurately an Act of Rights as it would be called should Parliament pass such legislation) is rather complicated. It is made worse with Britain not having a fully written and codified constitution. As with many of the conventions within the British constitution, the rights of the individual are not clarified.

Whereas a constitution is to do with "the rules of the political game", a Bill of Rights focuses upon individual freedoms, duties, rights and obligations. Most countries with written constitutions have a Bill of Rights, or some similar document, entrenched in the constitution. In this way, the Bill of Rights is protected within the constitution. Thus a government may not change the legislation on a whim. Currently, in Britain, the document which protects the rights of the individual is the Human Rights Act. This legislation was a manifesto commitment of the Labour Party during the 1997 General Election. It was enacted the following year, and was enforceable from October 2000.

A Bill of Rights

This document details the rights and freedoms of every individual. As well as this, it also covers the duties and obligations of each person. Traditionally, a Bill of Rights is part of a written constitution.

The Human Rights Act is based upon the European Convention of Human Rights. This document was written in the late 1940s and was ratified by the British Government in 1951. It was not incorporated into British law at the time because it was felt that such a rigid document might undermine the traditional flexibility of the British constitution. Tables 4.1 and 4.2 detail the Human Rights Act.

Table 4.1 The Rights and Freedoms included in the Human Rights Act 1998

Article	Title
2	Right to Life
3	Prohibition of Torture
4	Prohibition of Slavery and Forced Labour
5	Right to Liberty and Security
6	Right to a Fair Trial
7	No Punishment Without Law
8	Right to Respect for Private and Family Life
9	Freedom of Thought, Conscience and Religion
10	Freedom of Expression
11	Freedom of Assembly and Association
12	Right to Marry
14	Prohibition of Discrimination
16	Restrictions on Political Activity of Aliens
17	Prohibition of Abuse of Rights
18	Limitations on Use of Restrictions of Rights

Table 4.2 Protocols within the Human Rights Act 1998

Protocol	Article	Title
First Protocol	1	Protection of Property
	2	Right to Education
	3	Right to Free Elections
Sixth Protocol	1	Abolition of Death Penalty
	2	Death Penalty in Time of War

The Human Rights Act was considered to be a contentious piece of legislation. It effectively codified a number of rights that the British people thought that they had. This codification gives some degree of protection to the rights of an individual. However, the Human Rights Act can be suspended by the Home Secretary under certain circumstances. David Blunkett suspended the Human Rights Act after the attack on the World Trade Centre. This meant that anyone suspected of any related terrorist activities would not have the same protection of rights as the rest of the population.

As a consequence of these actions, calls for a proper Bill of Rights were resurrected. There is a line of argument which says that the Human Rights Act is not strong enough. It can be repealed by any subsequent government, and can be suspended on the whim of a government. Thus there is still a demand for a full Bill of Rights.

Does Britain Need a Bill of Rights?
The case in favour of a Bill of Rights

Until the enactment of the Human Rights Act in October 1998, there had been demand for a proper Bill of Rights for Britain from organisations such as Charter88. The Labour Government expected such demand to be dissipated with the Human Rights Act. Yet this has not been the case. One major argument is that the Human Rights Act is not comprehensive enough. While there is a very clear list of rights (as detailed in Tables 4.1 and 4.2), these are not protected. The legislation could be reversed by a subsequent government. It can also be suspended. In fact the possible suspension of the Human Rights Act is actually built into the document. In Article 9, which is entitled 'Freedom of Thought, Conscience and Religion', the second paragraph states:

> Freedom to manifest one's religion or beliefs shall be subject only
> to such limitations as are prescribed by law and are necessary in
> a democratic society in the interests of public safety, for the
> protection of public order, health or morals, or for the protection
> of the rights and freedoms of others

The interpretation of what is necessary is to be carried out by the courts. However, noting the doctrine of Parliamentary Sovereignty, it could be possible for Parliament to legislate to prevent such freedoms being exercised through very narrow interpretations of public order or morals. Thus Parliament could ignore or override the Human Rights Act.

Added to this, the government can suspend the Human Rights Act. Admittedly this is supposed to be during times of a public emergency.

Blunkett declared a formal state of emergency after the attack on the World Trade Centre. In doing so, he was able to suspend parts of the Human Rights Act. However, at the time, Blunkett admitted that "it isn't a real emergency. It's more like a technicality". An apparent justification was that the suspension of parts of the Human Rights Act would only apply to a few people, particularly foreign nationals suspected of involvement in terrorism. Nobody else would suffer from the extra monitoring of things such as the internet or mobile phone use. Even airlines and ferries were told to retain all records of passengers and freight. So it does seem that the Human Rights Act is not strong enough to protect our basic rights, and that an entrenched Bill of Rights is what is actually needed.

Linked to this has been the growth in executive power. Lord Hailsham's description of Britain's Parliamentary process as an 'elective dictatorship' is probably more accurate now than when he originally coined the phrase in 1976. The concept of 'Parliamentary sovereignty', which is supposed to be the underpinning of the British constitution, has succumbed to executive power strengthened by the supremacy of a party majority in the House of Commons. Stringent party discipline usually ensures that the government's will prevails. Even during the Major Government – particularly between 1992 and 1997 where the Conservative majority in the House of Commons started at 21 and gradually decreased – the Executive was able to force through the bulk of its' legislative programme. The Blair Government, with a majority of 165 after the 2001 General Election, had no problem whatsoever in dictating the Parliamentary agenda.

Yet it is not just in Parliament that Executive dominance can be seen. Margaret Thatcher wished to "roll back the frontiers of the State". She wanted to reduce the amount of government 'interference' in the running of the economy. However, whereas the direct running of the economy and the country as a whole may have been reduced, the indirect running – in areas such as regulation – has expanded dramatically. Thus there are numerous regulatory bodies such as OFWAT (water) and OFGAS (gas), and other bodies such as the Commission for Racial Equality, where the government plays an indirect role in running the country.

Added to this there is also the domination of the Prime Minister. While this subject will be addressed in a subsequent chapter, it is important to note the extent to which the prime minister can dominate the executive. Margaret Thatcher and Tony Blair are both presented as dominant prime ministers, with increases in both the power and prestige in their Offices. In fact the prime minister is often portrayed as being 'Presidential', such is the extent of their dominance of the Executive. (This specific issue is addressed in Chapter Six.) While it is more of a constitutional issue as to how the powers of the prime minister and the executive can be curbed, the protection of individual rights and freedoms through an entrenched Bill of Rights would also go some way to protecting the people of Britain from virtually unchecked executive power.

An important area for a Bill of Rights is the redress of grievances. There are significant differences in this area between countries which have an entrenched Bill of Rights within their constitution and those without. Even with the Human Rights Act, the emphasis upon the redress of grievances is weak. In Britain there are numerous ways of seeking redress of grievances (see Pyper (1996) for an excellent analysis of this area). These include MPs, the Ombudsman (who investigates maladministration), tribunals, the courts, and the Citizen's Charter (and other various charters). Yet with such an extensive list, it is not always clear as to which body should be sought out to assist in the redress of grievances. A Bill of Rights ought to clarify this. The Human Rights Act does go some way towards remedying the situation, with the emphasis upon the courts.

When examining the status of the US Bill of Rights, some important comparisons can be drawn with Britain. While there is the Human Rights Act in the UK, it is not very well known. By contrast, in the US, the teaching of the Declaration of Rights and the US constitution is a prominent feature of the American culture. It is not simply a lack of education in Britain, it seems to be a lack of interest. The British are sometimes portrayed by Australians and New Zealanders as 'whinging Poms' because the British are always complaining. However, it is very rare for the British to go any further than moaning (see Chapter One on Political Culture). By contrast, in the USA actions are quite often carried through with litigation because of the infringement of people's rights. It is not just knowledge and awareness of rights but also their protection. An entrenched Bill of Rights is very important but also needs an educative programme to run alongside it.

The case against a Bill of Rights

One of the main arguments against adopting a Bill of Rights (and was also used against the adoption of the Human Rights Act) is that such legislation is contrary to the British tradition. The flexibility of the British constitution would be lost if such legislation were adopted. Instead of being able to adapt to changing circumstances and values, the rights of the British people would become constrained within a constitutional straitjacket. It would become far more difficult to alter a particular clause or even discard a convention. An example from the USA highlights such a problem. Article 2 of the US Declaration of Rights gives every citizen of the USA the right to bear arms. Whenever there is any mention of changing this 'right' – in particular after every massacre of school children in the USA – organisations such as the National Rifle Association raise the spectre of everybody's rights being undermined by the government. Rather than focusing on the issue of the problems of guns, the NRA and other pro-gun organisations present any such proposed change as a fundamental attack on the entire US constitution.

Another argument against having a Bill of Rights is that it would undermine Parliamentary sovereignty. This is one of the cornerstones of the British constitution. Only Parliament can pass, amend or abolish laws. No Parliament can bind the actions of any of its successors. Yet such a principle would be jeopardised by a Bill of Rights. The claims in such a document would probably take precedence over Parliamentary law, although MPs would probably retain some rights to amend legislation where appropriate. The adoption of a Bill of Rights could undermine the role of Parliament. Is it right that over 800 years of parliamentary development should be checked on the dubious grounds that the power of the executive has increased too much? Rather than pinning hopes on such a document, better procedures in Parliament, and more effective forms of scrutiny would probably be far more effective in keeping a check on the executive. A simple constitutional change such as replacing the Simple Plurality electoral system would also have more impact on the powers of the executive.

The Human Rights Act is not quite so influential. While all legislation that is passed by Parliament must conform to the Human Rights Act, Parliament can suspend the Act when it needs to do so. This could occur, for example, during some sort of crisis such as a natural disaster or a time of war.

It must also be noted that the existence of a Bill of Rights does not guarantee that all rights and freedoms will be protected. The former Soviet Union claimed to have the most democratic constitution in the world based on written guarantees, yet it did not really equate with western liberal expectations. Such concerns do not just apply to totalitarian regimes. Even the USA has suspended the constitutional rights for some of its citizens. To present two notable examples of such actions: the internment of Japanese Americans during the Second World War; and the discrimination and segregation laws against blacks throughout most of the twentieth century. In effect, a written constitution with an entrenched Bill of Rights does not mean that the basic freedoms expected in a western liberal society can be upheld.

The existence of the Human Rights Act is in itself a reason why a Bill of Rights is unnecessary. There is no need for two such documents. Although the Human Rights Act is not entrenched in the constitution, it is highly unlikely that any government would dare repeal such legislation. Even when the Human Rights Act has been suspended there has been an outcry from civil liberties organisations. Thus the codification of the rights of the British people has already occurred. In fact, the lack of entrenchment may provide the opportunity for Parliament to amend and update the document as society evolves. The Human Rights Act could actually present the best of both systems: a clear codification of rights for everyone to know and the flexibility to update such a document when needed.

A final concern about a Bill of Rights – and also the Human Rights Act – is in relation to the role of judges. This can be highlighted on two counts. The first is the potential politicization of the judiciary. Currently, all senior judicial appointments are made by the Monarch on the advice of both the Prime Minister and the Lord Chancellor. Thus there is already the chance for some politicisation. However, in March 2001, the Commission for Judicial Appointments was established. This body audits judicial appointments, through such processes as sitting in on interviews in an observer capacity. However, with a full Bill of Rights, the judicial process will come under mounting pressure, not least of which would be politicians. Even the proposed restructuring of the Law Lords into some form of a Supreme Court may not alleviate the situation.

A second concern about judges is the extent to which they are representative of society, or even in touch with ordinary people. Surveys in 1999 found a widespread lack of confidence in the fairness of the courts. These surveys also questioned the impartiality of judges. Even by 2002, the senior judiciary was perceived as white, male and public school–educated. To this list can also be added the label 'elderly', with accusations of judges "nodding off" during trials. The appointment of Dame Brenda Hale as the first female Law Lord may be viewed as little more than tokenism, but it could also be perceived as the first step in a more representative direction.

Awareness of popular culture or people also seems to be lacking. A case in point was Lord Justice Harman who expressed ignorance of someone or something called Gazza, except in relation to a Rossini opera. Clearly famous English footballers – or possibly even the sport of football itself – may be an anathema to many judges. With these perspectives on judges (although the more generous may describe them as isolated), it is hardly surprising that potential judicial rulings on a Bill of Rights may hold little faith.

Conclusion

As noted in the introduction to this chapter, the Labour Government hoped to deflect demand for an entrenched Bill of Rights by passing the Human Rights Act in 1998. To some extent this was successful as people are now able to find out about their rights in a simple codified document. However, the demand for a proper Bill of Rights has not disappeared. When examining such demand for a Bill of Rights, the arguments appear to hinge upon the extent to which the current Human Rights Act provides insufficient coverage of peoples' rights. As noted above, the existence of a Bill of Rights – or for that matter the Human Rights Act – is not in itself a guarantee that all rights will be respected. Yet any further movement on entrenching the Human Rights Act or adopting a Bill of Rights will be linked to further constitutional reform, and in particular the possible codification of the British constitution.

Summary of key points

DEFINITION OF A BILL OF RIGHTS

❑ This is a document which focuses on the rights and freedoms of the individual

❑ There are also duties and obligations that each individual has to fulfil as well

❑ Traditionally, a Bill of Rights is built into a written constitution

THE CASE IN FAVOUR OF A BILL OR RIGHTS

❑ The Human Rights Act (1998) can be suspended at any time (and has been)

❑ Parliament can reverse the Human Rights Act at any time (Parliamentary sovereignty)

❑ Limited redress of grievances under the current legislation

THE CASE AGAINST A BILL OF RIGHTS

❑ Such legislation would undermine Parliamentary sovereignty

❑ Repressive regimes such as the USSR had a Bill of Rights but this did not guarantee individual rights and freedoms

❑ The Human Rights Act (1998) covers everyone's rights

Further Reading

Elvidge, V.; "Elective Dictatorship" *Talking Politics* vol. 5, 1992

Hailsham, Lord; "Elective Dictatorship" *The Listener* 26 October 1976

Jowell, J. and Oliver, D. (eds.); *The Changing Constitution* (Oxford University Press, 2000, fourth edition)

Loveland, I.; *Constitutional Law, Administrative Law and Human Rights: A Critical Introduction* (LexisNexis, 2003)

Pyper, R. (ed.); *Aspects of Accountability: The British System of Government* (Tudor, 1996)

Woodhouse, D.; "The Law and Politics: In the Shadow of the Human Rights Act" *Parliamentary Affairs* vol. 55, 2002

Zander, M.; *A Bill of Rights?* (Sweet and Maxwell, 1997)

Internet Sites

www.charter88.org.uk

Charter88 homepage

www.hrcr.org/

Human and Constitutional Rights Homepage, from the Columbia Law School

www.lcd.gov.uk/hract/hramenu.htm

The Human Rights Unit, which is part of the Lord Chancellors Department

www.lcd.gov.uk/judicial/judgesfr.htm#part1

Information about judges and judicial appointments at the Lord Chancellors Department

www.legislation.hmso.gov.uk/acts/acts1998/19980042.htm

Human Rights Act 1998

www.ucl.ac.uk/constitution-unit

Homepage of the Constitution Unit, based at University College London

CHAPTER FIVE

Parliament

INTRODUCTION

The British Parliament comprises three parts: the House of Commons, the House of Lords and the Monarchy. Collectively, they are known as Parliament. However, a common mistake made by many students is to equate the term 'Parliament' solely with the House of Commons. While the House of Commons is by far the most powerful part of Parliament, it is important to note that all legislative proposals must be accepted by all three components to become law. The legislative process of the British Parliament is detailed in Table 5.1.

Parliament is not simply a legislative or law making body. It also performs a number of other roles. These include scrutiny, debating and representation.

Parliament

Parliament is the supreme law making body in the United Kingdom. It comprises three bodies: the House of Commons, the House of Lords and the Monarchy. Of these, the House of Commons is by far the most powerful body. As well as law making, Parliament has other roles, including: representing the people, and scrutinising the Executive.

Representation is often considered to be a very important role for the House of Commons. Each MP is directly elected from a single member constituency. The MP 'represents' all of his or her constituency members. However, an MP is also a party representative. In fact, in many cases, the party that the MP represents is often better known than the MP. Very few people tend to know what issues or beliefs their MP holds. However, they are more likely to know where the MPs' party stands on particular issues. Thus there may be problems for MPs with regard to who they actually represent. This issue is complicated still further when taking into consideration other areas such as an MPs profession, or their sponsors. Many MPs are sponsored by trade unions or business organisations, and are likely to have worked in a particular profession.

What happens when all of these conflict? Who does the MP represent then? In most cases, MPs will stand by their party ahead of their constituency or sponsor. Yet on issues such as Iraq, many MPs appeared rather unwilling to 'toe the party line'.

Table 5.1 The Legislative Process

House of Commons	First Reading	Introduce the bill
	Second Reading	Debate and vote on the thinking behind the bill
	Committee Stage	A Standing Committee, comprising MPs from all parties works through the detail of the legislation
	Report Stage	Report of Standing Committee
	Third Reading	Debate and vote on the text of the legislation
House of Lords	Accept legislation	Goes straight to Royal Assent
	Finance legislation	No opportunity to change the legislation. Straight to Royal Assent
	Amend legislation	Amendments may be proposed. They go to the Commons Standing Committee. If accepted, straight to Royal Assent. If not the legislation is delayed for up to one year before going for Royal Assent
Monarchy	Royal Assent	

The idea of debating tends to cover the role of both MPs and members of the House of Lords in their respective chambers. This is simply the idea of participating in debates in the House. MPs are likely to participate in debates that have an impact upon their constituents. This could include rather mundane matters such as building new roads in their constituency, closure of rural Post Offices, and other such matters, or more controversial ones such as housing asylum seekers. MPs and members of the House of Lords also participate in debates in which they may have an active interest. Thus former school teachers are likely to speak in any debate on the education system.

Linked to participating in debates is voting in Parliament. MPs are expected to vote with their party on most issues. This is because most votes (in both Houses) tend to be 'whipped'. A one-line whip means that attendance for voting is requested. A two-line whip means that attendance is expected. Finally, a three-line whip is the most important of all. Any MPs who defy a three-line whip can expect to be disciplined by their party. The most extreme sanction against MPs who defy a three-line whip could be deselection by their party. This means that an MP would not be able to stand as a representative of their party at the next general election. A counter-example here was when121 Labour MPs defied a three-line whip on Iraq in February 2003. Their vast number meant that they suffered very little fallout from the party or their constituencies.

The final role of both MPs and members of the House of Lords is scrutiny of the Executive. This role includes asking questions of Government Ministers or the Prime Minister at Question Time. MPs can also sit on select committees (see Table 5.2). These bodies may investigate particular issues. Departmental select committees shadow Government Departments. Select committees can ask questions of ministers, civil servants, or even members of the public. They are considered to be an essential part of the scrutiny of the Government. Unfortunately, there have been allegations of the party whips attempting to influence members of select committees. These bodies are supposed to be impartial in their scrutiny. If it is not the case, then they may no longer be an appropriate form of scrutiny.

Thus we can see that Parliament performs a number of roles. However, the strength of the political parties – and specifically the role of the party whips – suggests that Parliament may no longer be performing all of its various roles adequately. In fact there is a strong line of argument that Parliament ought to be reformed.

Does Parliament Need Reforming?

The case in favour of reform

When examining the case in favour of reforming Parliament, it is important to divide Parliament into its component parts. Thus in this section of the chapter, the House of Lords, the House of Commons and the Monarchy will each be examined.

Table 5.2 Select Committees (July 2004)

TYPES OF SELECT COMMITTEE	TITLE OF SELECT COMMITTEE (Number of members)	CHAIR OF SELECT COMMITTEE (Party)
DEPARTMENTAL	Constitutional Affairs (11)	Alan Beith (Lib Dem)
	Culture, Media and Sport (11)	Sir Gerald Kaufman (Lab)
	Defence (11)	Bruce George (Lab)
	Education and Skills (11)	Barry Sheerman (Lab)
	Environment, Food & Rural Affairs (17)	Michael Jack (Con)
	Foreign Affairs (11)	Donald Anderson (Lab)
	Health (11)	David Hinchcliffe (Lab)
	Home Affairs (11)	John Denham (Lab)
	International Development (11)	Tony Baldry (Con)
	Northern Ireland Affairs (13)	Michael Mates (Con)
	Office of Deputy Prime Minister (11)	Andrew Bennett (Lab)
	Science & Technology (11)	Dr Ian Gibson (Lab)
	Scottish Affairs (11)	Irene Adams (Lab)
	Trade and Industry (11)	Roger Berry (Lab)
	Transport (11)	Gwyneth Dunwoody (Lab)
	Treasury (11)	John McFall (Lab)
	Welsh Affairs (11)	Martyn Jones (Lab)
	Work and Pensions (11)	Sir Archy Kirkwood (Lib Dem)
SCRUTINY	European (14)	Jimmy Hood (Lab)
	Regulatory Reform (16)	Peter L Pike (Lab)
	Statutory Instruments (7)	David Tredinnick (Con)
JOINT (Membership is from both Houses)	Human Rights (12)	Jean Corston (Lab)
	Lords Reform (24)	Jack Cunningham (Lab)
	Statutory Instruments (14)	David Tredinnick (Con)
DOMESTIC (General running of the House)	Accommodation and Works (9)	Derek Conway (Con)
	Administration (9)	Marion Roe (Con)
	Broadcasting (10)	David Lepper (Lab)
	Catering (9)	Dennis Turner (Lab)
	Information (9)	Michael Fabricant (Con)
EXTERNAL MATTERS	Environmental Audit (16)	Peter Ainsworth (Con)
	Public Accounts (15)	Edward Leigh (Con)
	Public Administration (11)	Dr Tony Wright (Lab)
OTHERS	Finance and Services (11)	Stuart Bell (Lab)
	Liaison (Heads of Select Committees) (36)	Alan Williams (Lab)
	Modernisation (15)	Peter Hain (Lab)
	Procedure (13)	Sir Nicholas Winterton (Con)
	Standards and Privileges (10)	Sir George Young (Con)
	Selection (9)	John McWilliam (Lab)
	Chairman's Panel (31)	Sir Alan Haselhurst (Con)

The case for reforming the House of Lords is very clear. The reform process that began with the Wakeham Commission on the reform of the second chamber is still incomplete. Currently the House of Lords is full of appointed peers and hereditary peers. Although the 92 hereditary peers may claim some democratic legitimacy having been elected by their former colleagues in this chamber, the reality is that no member of the House of Lords has been elected by the general public. Thus the most obvious example of the need for the reform of the House of Lords is that it should be an elected chamber.

The Wakeham Commission acknowledged that there should be a directly elected element in a revised second chamber. However, the commission presented this proposal in a rather vague manner. In February 2003, Parliament was able to vote on the extent to which the House of Lords should be elected. Unsurprisingly, the Lords voted for a totally appointed chamber (which was the option that Tony Blair also supported). In the Commons, there were a range of options from totally appointed, 20% elected, 40% elected, 50% elected, 60% elected, 80% elected or totally elected. Each of these options was defeated in the Commons. For now, the status quo remains.

When the Wakeham Commission was established, one area that was beyond their remit was the powers of a second chamber. There is a fear in Britain that an elected second chamber could become an obstacle to the power of the House of Commons. Thus any reformed House of Lords will remain no more than a revising chamber. This is an opportunity lost. The powers of a revised second chamber needed to be re-examined. Currently, the House of Commons is dominated by political parties. Any government with a sizeable majority can force any legislative proposals through both Houses of Parliament. Thus flawed legislation appears on the statute books. Examples include the Dangerous Dogs Act, and even the Official Secrets Act. A more powerful second chamber could possibly prevent such legislative errors. However, it would also need to be accountable to the public. Critics of such ideas, such as Eric Forth, present the idea of gridlock. This is where in the possible event of different parties controlling different chambers, legislative proposals may pass from one chamber back to the other and no legislation is passed. The example of the USA is often cited, with the Democrats controlling one house and the Republicans the other. Yet, an alternative perspective of a similar scenario is to look to France. There have been Gaullist Presidents with Socialist Prime Ministers (most recently, Chirac and Jospin). Rather than gridlock, there was co-habitation. The opposing parties were compelled to work together.

A further alternative to reforming the House of Lords is to abolish it. There was a similar situation in New Zealand in 1950, where an appointed second chamber was simply abolished through an Act of Parliament. This would concentrate power even more in the remaining chamber – as is the case in

New Zealand – but such an action would eliminate the role of appointed and hereditary peers. Such a proposal has been included in most Labour Party election manifestos, at least until the leadership of Tony Blair. Yet even when elected to Office, the Labour Party never executed such actions.

Reform of the House of Commons is also very important. Currently it is undergoing what has been described as 'modernisation', but this is not enough. Much of the modernisation can be viewed as simply tinkering with the status quo. Changes to the hours of sitting or to the format of Prime Minister's Question Time are hardly radical. Yet much of the so-called modernisation is little more than this.

One area of reform that is needed is in the electoral system. While this is examined in greater detail in Chapter Eleven, it is also worthy of note here. Currently, MPs are elected under the Simple Plurality system (sometimes referred to as First-Past-the-Post). This means that MPs are elected in single member constituencies by a simple majority of votes. Whichever candidate wins the most votes is declared the winner. It is actually possible to be elected on around a quarter of the votes cast, as can be seen in Table 5.3.

Table 5.3 Result from Inverness East, Nairn and Lochaber (1992 General Election)

Candidate	Party	Votes	% votes
Sir D R Johnston	Liberal Democrat	13 258	26.0
D J Stewart	Labour	12 800	25.2
F S Ewing	SNP	12 562	24.7
J Scott	Conservative	11 517	22.6
J Martin	Green	766	1.5

Liberal Democrats win the constituency with a majority of 458 votes

What this means is that most parties that win elections do so on a minority of the vote. The last occasion where a party won a general election with over 50% of the votes cast was in 1935. Thus it could be argued that election results are not representative of the people. Such a criticism has been raised by the Liberal Democrats in all of their various guises. It is possible for a party to win over a quarter of all votes cast but very few seats. In the 1983 General Election, the Alliance won 25.4% of the vote but only 23 seats. In the same election, Labour won 27.6% of the vote and 209 seats. The problem here for minor parties is that votes are non-transferable. They are only valid in the constituency in which they are cast. With single member constituencies it is a winner–takes–all system.

From the perspective of the voter, choice is very limited in a general election. Voters may cast a single categoric choice i.e. a mark next to the candidate of their choice. This contrasts with other electoral systems where voters may rank candidates in order of preference or cast multiple votes. Added to this is the possibility of using multi-member constituencies which would potentially broaden the choice available to the voters.

Another area where reform is needed is in the legislative process. As demonstrated in Table 5.1, the current process is very cumbersome. Not only is it an antiquated process (counting heads in the lobby rather than using electronic voting), but it is also easily manipulated by the party whips. MPs who fail to toe the party line, particularly on important pieces of legislation, find themselves out in the cold. They may be shunned by their party colleagues, or possibly even deselected by their local constituency. The problem is to find ways in which the legislative process can be opened up. One option is to change the strictures for each reading of any legislative proposals. Why should debate be limited to the ideas behind the legislation in the Second Reading? Why must the debate focus solely upon the text of the legislation in the Third Reading?

The underlying problem is that the House of Commons is not really a legislature. Rather it legitimates the legislative proposals of the Government. The exception here is Private Members' Bills, but most of these tend to be defeated unless they have the support of the Government – for example the Abortion Bill in 1967. This legitimisation process is a direct consequence of the dominance of the party, and is clearly exemplified in the role of the party whips.

The consequence of the dominance of the party has been the concentration of power in the Executive. The control of the legislative process enables a government to pass its' legislative programme. Walter Bagehot observed in 1867 that the Monarchy and the House of Lords were 'dignified' parts of Parliament. They appeared powerful but were not. The House of Commons, on the other hand, was 'efficient' – it did not appear powerful but actually was. Since the latter part of the twentieth century, the Commons has become 'dignified'. Cabinet, or possibly even the Prime Minister alone, may be viewed as efficient. The role of Parliament has become that of a legislative rubber stamp. It is very rare indeed for Parliament to stand up to the Executive. The House of Commons has attempted to stand up to the Blair Government on a regular basis during 2003 – the war on Iraq, reform of the House of Lords, foundation hospitals, and fox hunting. Yet it was only on fox hunting (which was a free vote) that the Government was actually defeated. Thus what is needed is to find ways and means by which Parliament can hold the Executive to account for their actions. Procedures such as Prime Ministers' Question Time are largely theatrical – part of the dignified operation of Parliament. Bodies such as select committees are more successful in holding the Executive to account. However, they need their powers to be strengthened. While a select committee may be able to call for any person or document, even they sometimes feel the influence of the party whips calling their members to order. While such action or influence is deemed unacceptable, the fact of the matter is that it does occur. An example of such interference was in July 2001 when the Labour Party whips attempted to remove two independent-minded MPs - Gwyneth Dunwoody (Transport) and Donald Anderson (Foreign Affairs) – from their respective committees. Such was the backlash from this action that the two MPs were reinstated.

The final part of Parliament that is in need of reform is the Monarchy. While some steps have been taken to modernize the Monarchy, it is still a largely outdated institution. Calls for its' abolition will fall foul of the 1848 Treason Felony Act which make such calls an offence. This leaves reform.

There have been some moves to reform the Monarchy but arguably they are incomplete. The most notable step has been the paying of taxes, which the Monarch has voluntarily paid since 1993. The Monarch must also pay inheritance tax, but exempt from this are any transfers from Monarch to Monarch (and this included the Queen Mother). Another reform has been the Civil List. This is the amount of money voted by Parliament for the Monarch (currently £7.9 million per year). This is fixed until 2010, when it will next be reviewed. Included in the Civil List are the Duke of Edinburgh and other Royals. However, with the exception of the Duke of Edinburgh, the Monarch voluntarily repays any moneys in the Civil List for other Royals. As of the year 2000, the Monarch had accrued a surplus of £35 million from moneys granted through the Civil List. Supporters of further reform present this as an example of the excesses that the Monarchy currently enjoys.

The case against reform

The case against the reform of Parliament can be divided into the three separate parts of Parliament. In this way, each part can be analysed more clearly. When examining the case against reforming the House of Commons, there are two possible strands of argument. The first is that the status quo is fine and that no reform is needed. The alternative, and this appears to be the current position of the Blair Government, is that modernisation is needed. Each of these perspectives will be examined.

Any opposition to reforming the House of Commons highlights the extent to which Parliament as a whole has worked effectively and efficiently throughout its' existence. The methods of legislation and scrutiny have stood the test of time. Reform, or even modernisation, would be tampering with Parliamentary structures and processes for the sake of change rather than for any practical reason. When people vote for their MP, they are also voting for a government. The current electoral system encourages such a perspective. To support the idea of voting for a government is the need for a strong Executive that can push its legislative programme through Parliament. Within this, there are opportunities for all MPs and political parties to influence the legislation – in particular through Parliamentary debates, but also during the Standing Committee stage of the legislative process (see Table 5.1).

Although there is opposition to change, some developments have been given cross-party support in Parliament. The most notable development has been the Committee on Standards in Public Life. This committee was established in October 1994 in response to the allegations of misconduct and unethical behaviour among a number of politicians. Much of this came under the broad label of "sleaze". There were allegations of MPs taking cash in return for asking questions in Parliament. The Committee on Standards in Public Life was an attempt to restore public confidence in politicians, especially after the conduct of, among others, Neil Hamilton (former MP for Tatton). Thus this development was not seen as a reform of Parliament, or even some form of modernisation. Rather, it was a means to make sure that all MPs were worthy of the title "honourable member".

The current government does not appear overly keen on reform of the House of Commons. While Leader of the House, Robin Cook was enthusiastic in attempting to modernise the House of Commons. He focused on many of the little things, such as the hours of sitting. From January 2003, these have been changed to: Mondays 2:30pm to 10:30pm, Tuesdays and Wednesdays 11:30am to 7:30pm, Thursdays 11:30am to 6:30pm and on thirteen Fridays each year (although there are no set hours). The objective is to develop the House of Commons into a body that can operate effectively and efficiently in the 21st century. Thus MPs now have adequate office space with the opening of Portcullis House, which is opposite the Houses of Parliament. Added to this, the Commons also sits in Westminster Hall. On Tuesdays and Wednesdays (9:30am to 11:30am and 2pm to 4:30pm) Private Members Adjournment debates are held. These enable an MP to pursue a subject that has been unsatisfactorily dealt with at Question Time, or to raise a particular concern or grievance on behalf of a constituent. On Thursdays (2:30pm to 5:30pm) select committee reports are heard and debated. Another change has been to move Prime Minister's Question Time from 2:30pm to 11:30am every Wednesday.

All of these steps in the modernisation process are based on the loose premise that the House of Commons is relatively good in what it does. There is simply a need to make it a little more family friendly in such things as the hours of sitting. What was surprising was the level of opposition to such a move. Some of it, according to Andrew Mackinlay (Labour MP for Thurrock) was to do with ministers trying to avoid questions. Government ministers were hiding behind the "family friendly" mantra.

Other aspects of modernisation that could be introduced include a crèche within Parliament. Currently there are no such child care facilities. Instead there are such facilities as a gymnasium and a gun club. When a proposal for a crèche was raised in January 1995, the response from Dame Jill Knight was that there was insufficient room for such a facility.

The case against reform of Parliament can also be directed towards the House of Lords. As with the Commons, there are two separate strands. The first is that reform is not needed but abolition is a better alternative. The other is that the Chamber is very effective as it is and needs no reform. Some reform has already taken place and it is more than enough.

As noted earlier in this chapter, there is still support for the abolition of the second chamber. Such a body was abolished in New Zealand in 1950. There is no need for a second chamber, especially in its current form – a group of appointed people who are likely to carry out the Prime Minister's bidding. Even if the body was to be directly elected, it would still perform an inadequate role. All suggestions of reform to date have been based upon the primacy of the House of Commons, leaving the House of Lords (in whatever form) as no more than a revising chamber which can be ignored. Yet were a reformed second chamber to be given powers to challenge the House of Commons, there could easily be a power struggle between the two bodies. Which body's decisions should take precedence? Rather than working through a range of mundane arguments, it would be far easier to abolish the House of Lords and concentrate on giving the Commons the power to scrutinise the Executive properly.

The alternative line when arguing against reforming the House of Lords is to point out that there have already been significant changes to this body and that it now performs its' role more than adequately. There is no need for further reform. The hereditary peers have been removed – all bar a rump of 92 who were elected by their colleagues. A process is being undertaken to examine the possibility of having some members of the House of Lords elected by the public. This process is ongoing as the Commons could not reach an agreement on how many members of the revised second chamber ought to be elected.

Lord Wakeham chaired a Commission which conducted a review of the House of Lords in 2000. His report presented a number of proposals for reform. These are detailed in Table 5.4. In effect, Wakeham's report proposed to make the reformed second chamber more representative of society on the grounds of ethnicity, gender and religion, with the power to appoint membership removed from the powers of the Prime Minister. Links between Honours and the House of Lords were also to be dropped. There has also been the creation of People's Peers. Members of the public were encouraged to put themselves forward to be representatives in the reformed Chamber. To date fifteen such peers have been appointed, although more are expected in 2004, although further reform to the House of Lords appears to be on hold at the moment. The fifteen were selected by a special commission that was established for this very purpose.

Table 5.4 Wakeham Report Proposals

❑ Second Chamber to contain around 550 members

❑ An independent commission to select most members

❑ Some members to be elected (on a regional basis)

❑ Composition of chamber to be regularly readjusted to reflect voting patterns

❑ Targets to reflect the UK population by gender, ethnicity and religious denomination

❑ Links between Honours List and membership of the chamber to be dropped

❑ Powers of the chamber to be no less than those currently wielded by the Lords

In effect, the reforms of the Lords, as proposed by Lord Wakeham and his committee, leave the chamber as a revising body. If there is a strong Opposition to the Government in the House of Commons, then it is likely that the role of the second chamber will be limited. However, during times of weak Opposition, when the Government has an insurmountable majority in the Commons, the reformed Chamber will act as a counterbalance to the potential elective dictatorship in the Commons. This has been evident after both the 1997 and 2001 General Elections, when the only effective opposition to the Blair Government seems to come from the House of Lords. One of the most prominent examples of such opposition was over the change in electoral system for the British elections to the European Parliament. On seven occasions the House of Lords refused to accept the Commons' proposal for closed party lists (see Chapter Eleven for a comprehensive explanation of this type of list) arguing that they did not fit in with the British tradition of the voter casting his or her ballot for an individual. Ultimately, the Lords backed down, but a public debate was started over how people should be able to cast their ballots. This was a consequence of the House of Lords' actions. The House of Commons had been largely impotent in attempting to block the Blair Governments proposal for closed lists, or even generating a public debate on the subject. It is during such times that a body which is independent of the Prime Minister may well come into its' own.

The final part of Parliament is the Monarchy. As with the House of Lords, the argument against reform is either supportive of outright abolition, or, conversely, that we should leave well alone. The argument for abolition has already been mentioned in this chapter. In effect do we want the current incumbent and her successors as Head of State or not. If the latter, then who should replace the Monarch? The most prominent suggestion has been to have a directly elected Head of State. Yet, if this was to happen, the question then becomes one of what powers should that person wield? The Republic of Ireland has a President as Head of State (currently Mary McAleese), whose role is that of a figurehead. Arguably, this is less than the current role of the British Monarch. Yet some of the powers wielded by the Monarch, such as the dissolution of Parliament, could be removed altogether. This specific example would entail the creation of fixed-term Parliaments.

The alternative position is to leave the Monarchy alone. The Royal Family is supposed to symbolise the United Kingdom of Great Britain and Northern Ireland, as well as the entire Commonwealth. There has been some reform of the Monarchy, such as the paying of taxes. However, anything more radical may actually undermine the entire Parliamentary system and the British constitution as well. The phrase 'Queen in Parliament' is the formal title of the British legislature, which comprises the sovereign, the House of Lords and the House of Commons. Its most obvious example is in the State Opening of Parliament, with the Queen's Speech. All of this pageantry is beamed to the rest of the world.

Conclusion

The British Parliament is often described as the 'Mother of all Parliaments'. It is one of the oldest such bodies still in existence today. The problem appears to be that its methods of operating have not evolved. There is an emphasis upon tradition and continuity. Whenever a suggestion of reform or change is presented there is an outcry, with accusations of attempts to undermine Parliament. With this dogged opposition to reform, a piecemeal approach has been adopted. Thus in the Commons there is some form of ongoing modernisation. The processes are tinkered with, as a stepping stone towards greater reform. In the Lords there has been reform − at least in that most hereditary peers are no longer involved. However, this was supposed to be the first step in the reform process. The problem is that there appears to be little political will to take the process any further. This leaves the Monarchy. Calls for its reform or abolition tend not to be broadcast or published. In February 2001, the *Guardian* newspaper published a number of articles challenging the Treason Felony Act of 1848 which makes it a criminal offence to advocate the abolition of the monarchy. The case was thrown out. Suggestions of reform also tend to fall on deaf ears. Thus the British Parliament, as a whole, continues to endure. It may be the Mother of all Parliaments but it is in need of revitalising. The problem, noting the levels of intransigence, remains how it is to be done.

Summary of key points

DEFINITION OF PARLIAMENT

❑ Parliament comprises three bodies: the House of Commons, the House of Lords and the Monarchy

❑ Constitutionally, Parliament is the supreme law making body in the UK

❑ Parliaments other roles include scrutiny of the Executive and representation of the people

THE CASE IN FAVOUR OF REFORM OF PARLIAMENT

❑ Reform of the Lords
  ▫ Hereditary and appointed peers, who are unaccountable to the people, are involved in the legislative process
  ▫ What powers should a reformed second chamber wield?
  ▫ Abolition of the Chamber rather than reform?

❑ Reform of the Commons
  ▫ 'Modernisation' is not enough
  ▫ Domination of parties
  ▫ Power of the Executive (use of Party Whips)

❑ Reform of the Monarchy
  ▫ An out-dated, unaccountable institution
  ▫ Replace it with an elected figurehead
  ▫ The cost of the Monarchy and the Civil List to the tax payer

THE CASE AGAINST REFORM OF PARLIAMENT

❏   Reform of the Lords

    ▫   Abolition rather than reform needed

    ▫   Sufficient reforms have already been carried through

    ▫   More representative of the people e.g. People's Peers

❏   Reform of the Commons

    ▫   Merely in need of 'modernisation' rather than wholesale reform

    ▫   The Commons is evolving e.g. hours of sitting changed and Prime Ministers Questions moved

    ▫   Committee on Standards in Public Life has combated sleaze successfully

❏   Reform of the Monarchy

    ▫   Abolition rather than reform

    ▫   A symbol of the United Kingdom and the Commonwealth

Further Reading

Cowley, P.; "The Commons: Mr Blair's Lapdog?" *Parliamentary Affairs* vol. 54, 2001

Cowley, P. and Stuart, M.; "Parliament: Mostly Continuity, But More Change Than You'd Think" *Parliamentary Affairs* vol. 55, 2002

Norton, P.; "Parliament in Transition" in Pyper, R. and Robins, L. (eds.); *United Kingdom Governance* (St. Martins Press, 2000)

Norton, P.; "Would fixed-term Parliaments enhance democracy?" in Robins, L. and Jones, B. (eds.) *Debates in British Politics Today* (Manchester University Press, 2000)

Riddell, P.; *Parliament Under Blair* (Politico's Publishing, 2000)

Shell, D.; "Labour and the House of Lords" *Parliamentary Affairs* vol. 53, 2000

Silk, P. and Walters, R.; *How Parliament Works* (Longman, 1998, 4th edition)

Internet Sites

www.houseoflordsappointmentscommission.gov.uk

Full information on the House of Lords Appointments Commission

www.parliamentlive.tv/

Web page for live broadcasts in the House of Commons, House of Lords,

Westminster Hall and of select committees

www.parliament.uk

This is the best starting point for any investigation into the British Parliament.

www.politics.guardian.co.uk/lords/

The Guardian newspaper has a series of special reports on the Wakeham Commission and the reform of the House of Lords. Other newspapers have something similar.

www.royal.gov.uk

Homepage of the Monarchy

CHAPTER SIX

The Executive

INTRODUCTION

The executive is the apex of the British political system, comprising government ministers, the cabinet and the prime minister. The traditional perspective of the British Government focused upon Parliament, with ministers being selected from that august body. Today, the reality is significantly different. A general election is now a battle between potential governments – if not, more specifically, potential prime ministers. The legions of each political party parade their respective leaderships and the media laps it all up. A general election is now, at least in the eyes of the media, a battle to select the leadership of the country – a battle for someone to become the Prime Minister.

Executive

This is one of three branches of government – the others being the legislative and the judiciary. The Executive comprises the Prime Minister, the Cabinet, and Government ministers. It is the summit of the governmental structure. Its main role is policy formulation and decision making. Any laws required as a result of these decisions must be passed by the legislature (Parliament).

Cabinet

The 20 or so senior ministers in the Government. Each minister heads a government department, with the exception of the Prime Minister. The cabinet normally meets at least once a week.

Prime Minister

The chairperson of the Cabinet, the PM appoints all cabinet members and can promote or demote any member.

The focus upon the prime minister and the executive is quite interesting, especially from a constitutional perspective. Within the British constitution, there is no real provision for a prime minister. The role of the cabinet is acknowledged, and Bagehot even went as far as highlighting the need for a strong executive. Yet there was only limited mention of the role of the prime minister.

Regardless of this, the post of the prime minister has evolved over time. The first so-called Prime Minister was Robert Walpole. Yet the label was considered to be a term of derision rather than an acknowledgement of the position held. However, the powers wielded by the first prime minister are likely to bare little resemblance to those wielded by Tony Blair today or even any of his predecessors during the twentieth century (see the list of office holders in Table 6.1). Post-second world war, the powers of the prime minister have changed little. It has been the attitude of the post-holder that has largely determined how the powers have been wielded. Yet even this has depended upon a number of factors; most notably the size of the Parliamentary majority and the compliance of the Cabinet. A prime minister cannot govern alone. The post holder is dependent upon their political party, their cabinet and ministerial colleagues, and, in the words of Harold Macmillan, "events dear boy, events".

Yet it is only when the actual powers wielded by a prime minister are listed that it is possible to get an idea of the potential dominance of the post. A prime minister has the power of appointment. He or she has a free hand to choose their cabinet and all of the junior ministerial posts. The prime minister can hire and fire almost at will. Another power of appointment is to quangos and other such extra-governmental bodies. This particular topic is addressed in Chapter Eight. Added to this are knighthoods and other honours. The prime minister is also the leader of their political party. The success of any political party hinges upon their leader. Nothing helps to entrench support more than success. The prime minister has power over the people. In effect, elections are a form of 'beauty contest' between potential leaders. The winner gains power over the people, at least until the subsequent general election. This leads on to the final power – that of calling a general election. In theory, the prime minister asks the monarch to dissolve Parliament and call a general election. Such a request has not been refused.

Thus there is an extensive range of powers. These powers are available to every modern day prime minister. Yet no two prime ministers are the same. Some prime ministers dominate their cabinet (Thatcher and Blair); others are far more collegial (Douglas-Home and Major). Whenever a prime minister appears weak-willed, there are calls in the media for strong leadership. This was particularly the case during the Major Premiership, although to a degree, unfairly so. The converse is also true. When a prime minister appears to be too dominant, there are complaints that the prime minister may be ignoring the cabinet or, worse still, Parliament. In fact with a dominant prime minister, there is often the accusation that they are becoming 'presidential'. Graham Thomas asked "Has Prime Minister Major been replaced by President Blair?" The idea of a presidential Prime Minister is something that has built up over time during the Thatcher years as well as under Blair.

Table 6.1 British Prime Ministers during the twentieth century

Prime Minister	Party	Date of taking Office
The Marquis of Salisbury	Unionist (Conservative)	25 June 1895
Arthur Balfour	Unionist (Conservative)	12 July 1902
Sir Henry Campbell -Bannerman	Liberal	5 December 1906
Herbert Asquith	Liberal (1)	8 April 1908
David Lloyd George	Liberal (2)	7 December 1916
Andrew Bonar Law	Unionist (Conservative)	23 October 1922
Stanley Baldwin	Unionist (Conservative)	22 May 1923
Ramsay MacDonald	Labour	22 January 1924
Stanley Baldwin	Conservative	4 November 1924
Ramsay MacDonald	Labour	5 June 1929
Ramsay MacDonald	Labour (3)	24 August 1931
Stanley Baldwin	Conservative (3)	7 June 1935
Neville Chamberlain	Conservative (3)	28 May 1937
Winston Churchill	Conservative (4)	10 May 1940
Clement Attlee	Labour	26 July 1945
Sir Winston Churchill	Conservative	26 October 1951
Sir Anthony Eden	Conservative	6 April 1955
Harold Macmillan	Conservative	10 January 1957
Sir Alec Douglas-Home	Conservative	19 October 1963
Harold Wilson	Labour	16 October 1964
Edward Heath	Conservative	19 June 1970
Harold Wilson	Labour	4 March 1974
James Callaghan	Labour	5 April 1976
Margaret Thatcher	Conservative	4 May 1979
John Major	Conservative	18 November 1990
Tony Blair	Labour	1 May 1997

Notes: (1) Coalition Government from 1915

(2) Coalition Government

(3) National Government

(4) Coalition Government from May 1940 until May 1945; National Government from May 1945 until July 1945

Is there now a Presidential Prime Minister?

The case in favour of a Presidential Prime Minister

The suggestion that Britain now has a 'presidential' prime minister is not new. The label was used to describe the Thatcher Government of the 1980s, as well as the current Blair Government. The idea of a 'president' is linked to the United States, with both the British Prime Minister and the US President wielding similar powers and having posts of similar status. The concentration of the media also highlights this perspective. The British Prime Minister is placed upon a pedestal similar to that of the US President. Any problems, concerns or successes are all attributed to the prime minister, rightly or wrongly. In fact the British Prime Minister, like the US President, may actually symbolise the country.

The concentration of power in the post of the prime minister under Tony Blair was highlighted the 'presidentialisation' of the post. Blair, in a manner not dissimilar to that of Margaret Thatcher, appears to ride roughshod over his cabinet. The meetings themselves have been reduced to around 30 minutes in duration. Blair appears to make decisions and then inform the cabinet. A clear example of this was over the Millennium Dome. Blair, it is alleged, simply informed the cabinet of his decision to go ahead with the project.

Blair has actually downplayed the role of the cabinet. Although it does still meet, the reality is that Blair prefers to have one-to-one discussions, or bi-laterals, with individual ministers. In this way, he can get to grips with the issues or concerns of all of his ministers, and can have a finger in every pie. However, such an approach has led to the allegation of 'control freakery'. It is not just that Blair appears to want to know what is going on, but he has actually set up a process by which his Office has to be informed of any press statements being made prior to their release. This was fully detailed in the Ministerial Code which was issued by the Cabinet Office in July 1997 and updated in July 2001. Its' full title is "Ministerial Code: A Code of Conduct and Guidance on Procedures for Ministers". The important aspect of alleged control freakery comes in Part 8 under 'Ministers and the Presentation of Policy'. Paragraph 92 states:

> In order to ensure the effective presentation of government policy, all major interviews and media appearances, both print and broadcast, should be agreed with the No 10 Press Office before any commitments are entered into. The policy content of all major speeches, press releases and new policy initiatives should be cleared in good time with the No 10 Private Office. The timing and form of announcements should be cleared with the No 10 Strategic Communications Unit.

(www.cabinet-office.gov.uk/central/2001/mcode/contents.htm)

In effect, any policy proposals need to be cleared by the various parts of the Prime Ministers Office prior to their release. It could suggest that the Prime Minister is in a position to gag or block any proposals of which he does not approve.

Yet it is not just in the release of policy proposals that the heavy hand of the prime minister can be seen. It can also be seen in the formulation of policy. Through the use of special advisors, Blair is able to 'make' policy without necessarily consulting the actual department or cabinet minister. Such influence came to light when Estelle Morris resigned as Education Secretary in October 2001. It was suggested that Andrew Adonis, Blair's special enforcer on public services policy, put forward ideas that Blair was keen to adopt in the education sector, without any reference to Estelle Morris. The most prominent of these was university top up fees, especially noting Morris's lack of enthusiasm for such a policy. In effect, Adonis was the eyes and ears for the Prime Minister in a number of government departments. His job was to intrude and to report back to the Prime Minister. Yet his interference was always presented as some form of collaboration.

It is not just in education that Blair has a specific special advisor. He has special advisors in a number of other spheres, for example Lord Birt as his Transport supremo. This structure of government is very clearly modelled on the US system, where the US President has special advisors to cover all aspects of government. Although the President's Office is extensive, the Prime Minister's Office is small but growing in size and influence.

With such an extensive focus on the role of the prime minister particularly in the media, and the current incumbents' apparent desire to see all and know all, it is hardly surprising that the label 'presidential' is being applied. During the build up to the war against Iraq, Tony Blair strode the globe in an attempt to form a United Nations coalition to topple Saddam Hussein. He appeared willing to ignore the advice and opinions of his cabinet members (most notably Robin Cook who resigned), his party (with the largest ever rebellions against a governing party in a Parliamentary vote), and the millions of people around the UK and the world who marched in protest against the war. Blair's response was adamant. Important, difficult decisions had to be made. He had to make them. He would have preferred to have carried Parliament, party and public with him. However, in his opinion, his decision was the correct one. Others had the right to voice their opinions, and he respected them for doing just that. He had listened to them, now they should listen to him. But, ultimately, it was his decision. Blair stated on 21 February 2003:

All I ask people to do is understand that however sincerely they hold their view, I hold my view sincerely too. And there is another side to this argument. I understand exactly why people feel so strongly, but in the end, I have got to make a decision and that's the difference between leadership and commentary. I have got to make a decision.

The leader of Britain viewed everything as "his" decision. He may consult, he may listen. Yet Blair's role in the build up to the war against Iraq demonstrated very clearly the extent to which Britain now has a presidential prime minister.

The case against a Presidential Prime Minister

The idea of a 'presidential' prime minister is fundamentally flawed. While the prime minister may be able to give leadership to the country, and may be able to dominate both cabinet and Parliament, this does not mean that the post has become 'presidential'. The comparison is drawn with the President of the United States. Yet, in examining the two posts, there are very simple differences that demonstrate that the British Prime Minister is not presidential.

The first point to note is that the President of the United States is directly elected. Every person over the age of 18 who is on the electoral register can vote for a presidential candidate. Thus the president has a direct mandate from the American people – even if he fails to win the most votes as in the case of George W. Bush. The British Prime Minister, on the other hand, is not directly elected. The only people who may have any input are the party members who voted for their leader, and the constituents who voted for their MP. Thus Tony Blair was selected by the Labour Party as their leader and was elected by the people of Sedgefield to be their MP. Blair was dependent upon enough Labour MPs gaining election for him to become the Prime Minister.

The next point to note is that the US President has a free hand to select his cabinet and his senior civil servants, and if need be can appoint top judges and Supreme Court judges. All of these are political appointments that are within the gift of the President. The British Prime Minister, on the other hand, has a far more limited range of choices. Most cabinet members will come from the House of Commons, although appointments are also made from the House of Lords. Judicial appointments are not within the gift of the prime minister, but instead the Lord Chancellor (who is, admittedly, appointed by the Prime Minister) – although the judicial appointments process is being overhauled. Senior civil servant posts tend to be put up for open competition. The idea of a prime minister (Thatcher) asking "Is he one of us?" when appointing civil servants no longer exists (assuming it ever did).

Just from these areas alone, there are significant differences which highlight the extensive powers of the US President. Yet, at the same time, the British Prime Minister has power and influence of which a US president can only dream. The British Prime Minister is leader of their political party and is also a member of the legislature. This means that it is possible for the British Prime Minister to control the entire legislative process – especially so in the case of Tony Blair with a Commons majority of 165. In the USA there is a clear separation of powers between the Executive and the Legislative. A US president cannot force legislation through the House of Representatives and the Senate, although he can veto any proposals of which he does not approve. The president does not even sit in the legislature. This demonstrates clear differences between the post of president and prime minister. Already it ought to be clear that the British Prime Minister is not presidential.

Yet, even within the current cabinet, it is not clear as to how much control Tony Blair actually wields. All of his cabinets have been divided between those loyal to Blair and those loyal to the Chancellor of the Exchequer, Gordon Brown. Every cabinet reshuffle that Blair has carried out has seen media reports on the balance between Blairites and Brownites. Gordon Brown is portrayed as the Prime Minister in waiting. He wields more power within the cabinet than any other save Blair. No previous prime minister has ever tolerated such a rival power base within the cabinet. The media has revelled in the various Blairites that Gordon Brown has dispatched, including John Prescott, David Blunkett, Charles Clarke, Alan Milburn and Peter Mandelson. When examining issues such as when will Britain join the Euro, Blair bows to Brown. Brown has decreed that there are five economic tests that need to be passed before a referendum can be held. Blair has publicly accepted this position, and has not questioned his Chancellors decision, even though he still envisages Britain at the heart of Europe.

At the Parliamentary level, the dominance of the prime minister can be questioned – most notably over Iraq. Tony Blair has suffered the two largest Parliamentary rebellions ever during the Iraq crisis, as well as one over foundation hospitals. In fact, if it was not for the support of the Conservative MPs in the Commons particularly over Iraq, Blair's position as Prime Minister might actually have been under threat. On 26 February 2003, 122 Labour MPs defied a three line party whip and supported a motion that the case for military action had not been proven. All 52 Liberal Democrat MPs and 13 Conservative MPs also supported the motion. However, this meant that around 150 Conservative MPs actually supported the Prime Minister's position. The following month (18 March 2003), there was an even larger rebellion against Tony Blair on the very same issue, with 140 Labour MPs defying a three line whip. Although in each case the outcome gave Parliamentary support to Blair's position, a lot of it was due to Conservative

Party support.

Thus Tony Blair's position as a 'Presidential' Prime Minister must be questioned. While he does appear strutting the globe, committing Britain to military action without full United Nations support, he is doing so at great risk to himself and the post that he holds. A prime minister is not able to make all of the key decisions without support from their party, Parliament and Cabinet. There is a relationship of mutual dependence. It is even debatable as to whether Britain has 'Prime Ministerial' government. As Smith (1995, pp. 123–124) has noted:

> British government is not cabinet government or prime ministerial government. Cabinets and prime ministers act within the context of mutual dependence based on the exchange of resources with each other and with other actors and institutions within the core executive. A prime minister can only be dominant with the support or acquiescence of cabinet and attempts at dominance without this support undermine the relationships of dependence. The power of the prime minister varies greatly according to the issues, the external circumstances and the resources of other actors within the core executive.

Thus what can be seen in the British executive is the possibility of a dominant prime minister. However, such dominance is dependent upon the rest of the Executive. The last dominant Prime Minister, Margaret Thatcher, was toppled by her Cabinet. She had been described as 'Presidential' but her removal suggested otherwise. Blair's dominant position has been given a similar description but it is similarly inaccurate. A Prime Minister may be able to dominate his or her party, cabinet and Parliament, but that does not make them presidential. It makes them a leader or a figure head but not a president.

Conclusion

The idea of a presidential prime minister is not new. It is a label that has been attached to the two most powerful peacetime prime ministers to have led Britain. The label is used to describe the extent of their dominance. It is not accurate to describe either Thatcher or Blair as a president, but it is a useful, if somewhat inaccurate, to portray their respective positions as 'presidential'. This signifies the extent to which they have dominated not just their cabinet, party or even Parliament, but rather they way in which they have dominated British politics. Both hold strong convictions, and the belief that they are correct. This may be somewhat misguided, but very few people or politicians have been willing to stand up to either prime minister. Presidents they are not, but the label 'presidential' can be used to describe the extent of their power. But, as noted before, Margaret Thatcher was eventually removed from post by her cabinet. Tony Blair may need to beware.

Summary of key points

DEFINITION OF EXECUTIVE

❏   One of three branches of Government – the others are the Legislature and the Judiciary

❏   The main decision making and policy making body in Government

THE CASE FOR A PRESIDENTIAL PRIME MINISTER

❏   Concentration of Executive power in the Prime Minister

❏   The Prime Minister is able to dominate their Cabinet via their powers of patronage – the ability to promote or demote Ministers

❏   By-passing of Cabinet with use of bi-lateral meetings with ministers and use of Special Advisers

❏   All policy proposals to be cleared by the Prime Minister's Office

THE CASE AGAINST A PRESIDENTIAL PRIME MINISTER

❏   The Prime Minister is not directly elected to the post and is dependent upon a party majority in the Legislature

❏   Restraints on political, judicial and other appointments

❏   Other powerful members of the Executive are able to restrict some activities of the Prime Minister

Further Reading

Barbaris, P.; "Prime Minister and Cabinet" in Pyper, R. and Robins, L. (eds.); *United Kingdom Governance* (Macmillan, 2000)

Finlayson, A.; "Elements of the Blairite Image of Leadership" *Parliamentary Affairs* vol. 55, 2002

Heffernan, R.; "Prime ministerial predominance? Core executive politics in the UK" *British Journal of Politics and International Relations* vol. 5, 2003

Hennessy, P.; *The Prime Minister: The Office and its Holders since 1945* (Allen Lane, 2000)

Jackson, N.; "The Blair Style: Presidential, Bilateral or Trilateral Government?" *Talking Politics* vol. 15, 2003

McNaughton, N.; "Prime Ministerial Government" *Talking Politics* vol. 15-1, 2002

Smith, M.; "Interpreting the Rise and Fall of Margaret Thatcher: Power Dependence and the Core Executive" in Rhodes, R. and Dunleavy, P. (eds.); *Prime Minister, Cabinet and Core Executive* (Macmillan, 1995)

Thomas, G.; "Has Prime Minister Major been replaced by President Blair?" in Robins, L. and Jones, B. (eds.); *Debates in British Politics Today* (Manchester University Press, 2000)

Internet Sites

www.cabinet-office.gov.uk/central/index/mog.htm

The Cabinet Office page is where you can access information about ministers and departments. There is also information on the Ministerial Code, and a history of how government has been organised

www.number-ten.gov.uk/

Homepage of 10 Downing Street. From this page it is possible to access information on the Prime Minister and the Cabinet

www.open.gov.uk

UK online homepage

CHAPTER SEVEN

The Civil Service

INTRODUCTION

The civil service is often portrayed as the symbol of continuity within British politics. These employees of the government obey their political masters, carrying out their wishes unquestioningly, regardless of their own opinions. The standard caricature of a British civil servant has traditionally been of a white middle-aged, middle class man, who wore a pin striped suit and a bowler hat, carried a furled umbrella while walking to Whitehall, and who liked to drink tea. Such a caricature is still presented in films and on television today. Yet it could not be further from the truth. The age, gender and ethnicity perspectives are no longer quite so accurate, while only a sixth of civil servants actually work in Whitehall. The remainder are spread throughout the rest of the country. Tea is still a popular drink among civil servants.

Civil Servant

A servant of the Crown (or more accurately, the Government) who is employed in a civil capacity, and who is paid from central government funds.

Yet what is a civil servant? The generally agreed definition of a civil servant is one adapted from the Tomlin Commission (1931): "a person employed by the Crown, other than holders of political or judicial posts, to carry out the work of the Government in a civil capacity and who is paid completely and directly with money voted by Parliament". This definition covers approximately half a million employees divided into administrative, executive and clerical levels, along with scientists, lawyers, accountants, Customs and Excise Officers and other specialist sections of the civil service, as well as staff who work in the Executive Agencies (such as the Child Benefits Agency or the DVLA). The Tomlin definition excludes ministers and MPs, members of the armed forces, employees of Parliament, local government and NHS staff, employees of public corporations (such as the BBC), and members of quasi-governmental bodies. (The latter are examined in Chapter Eight).

The constitutional position of civil servants is that they obey the government of the day, regardless of political or ideological persuasion. However, there have been suggestions, particularly since the mid-1980s, that politicians have been unwilling to trust this constitutional perspective. Instead, it appears that successive governments have attempted to appoint 'like-minded' thinkers to senior civil service positions. Such action may be viewed as an important step towards the politicisation of the civil service.

Should the civil service be politicised?

The case against politicisation of the civil service

The constitutional position of civil servants is that they are neutral, impartial and anonymous. Politicians make the decisions, while civil servants implement them. The politicians are accountable to Parliament, while the civil servants are accountable to their superiors and, ultimately, to the minister. Civil servants obey the wishes of their political superiors. Yet a problem would appear to arise with a change of government, or even simply a change of minister. With a new politician in control, but the same civil servants in post, the minister needs to know that his/her decisions will be implemented. The formal constitutional position reinforces the neutrality of the civil servants. Civil servants are expected to be committed to the aims and objectives of the government of the day. Should there be a change in government, and with it a change in policies, the civil servants simply change their positions to conform to the new government.

Linked to this is the professionalism of the civil service. The integrity of the entire civil service could be placed at stake if an individual civil servant decided to follow personal opinion rather than that of the minister. The professionalism and integrity of the civil service are key features that would be undermined with any politicisation of the civil service. This is all part of the formal constitutional model of minister–civil servant relations. The role of civil servants is detailed in the Civil Service Code (see the website *www.cabinet-office.gov.uk/central/1999/cscode.htm*).

The idea of a non-politicised civil service is to avoid any attempt at partisan advantage with the civil service. Civil servants are not permitted to partake of party political matters. They focus upon government matters. While this line is often a little indistinct, it does serve as some form of a benchmark. Should ministers require political advice, rather than turning to their civil servants, they should turn to their special advisers. All ministers have special advisers. They have been a feature of ministerial support for many years, dating back to the 1960s. Even the television series Yes, Minister and Yes, Prime Minister had special advisers. The current government is awash with special advisers, to such an extent that a special code of conduct has been drafted to cover their actions. The Code of Conduct for Special Advisers states:

> ...the employment of special advisers on the one hand adds a political dimension to the advice available to Ministers, and on the other provides Ministers with the direct advice of distinguished experts in their professional field, while reinforcing the political neutrality of the permanent Civil Service by distinguishing the source of political advice and support

> Special advisers are employed to help Ministers on matters where the work of Government and the work of the Government Party overlap and it would be inappropriate for civil servants to become involved.

(Source: www.cabinet-office.gov.uk/central/2001/codconspads.htm)

Thus there is a clear distinction between sources of advice. Party political (or more accurately party-biased) advice will come from the special advisers. Civil servants present the neutral case, which is a presentation of facts with recommendations. Politicisation of the civil service would recreate the upper echelons of the civil service in the mould of the special advisers that are currently in use. It could also merge party political and governmental aspects of the role of civil servants.

In cases where there is a politicised civil service, problems often arise. An example would be the United States, which operates such a 'spoils' system. After each election, there are several thousand posts in the US bureaucracy within the gift of the president. One consequence of such patronage is discontinuity. There is a possibility of senior 'civil servants' being replaced every four years. Added to this, the personnel holding these posts have a simply objective of pleasing their political superiors. Rather than giving balanced advice with a recommendation, these senior 'civil servants' act in a manner more akin to special advisers than civil servants. It is very much a short term quick fix approach, rather than trying to establish some degree of expertise in the area.

This is not to say that the British model of bureaucracy is perfect. There are many flaws, including some that may appear in a politicised civil service, such as short-termism. The operations of the civil service are still loosely governed by the findings of the Northcote-Trevelyan Report (1854) which recognised the idea of a permanent civil service which owed its allegiance to the Crown. To ensure the highest quality of recruits, competitive examinations were introduced, with appointment and promotion on merit.

Moves have been taken by the last three British Prime Ministers to inject a more managerial approach towards the running of the civil service. It could be described as a process of modernisation of a body that has only gradually developed over the past 150 years. The Thatcher Government produced, among other things, the "Next Steps Report"; Majors' introduced the "Citizen's Charter"; the Blair Government has developed "Service First" and "Modernising Government". Each of these have taken steps to develop the civil service and to bring it into the twentieth (and twenty first) century. The current process is one of on-going modernisation and reform. The Next Steps Report has been refined by subsequent governments in an attempt to put a more 'human face' on the civil service – as if to remove the detachment that people may experience when dealing with the civil service. Arguably, it was a small step towards the privatisation of parts of the civil service, but it was not necessarily the politicisation of the civil service.

Possibly improvements could be made to the civil service without further politicisation of the organisation. Examples of where lessons may be learned can be seen in the civil service of France. The French civil service is based on two fundamental principles. The first is open access to all qualified people, based upon competitive examinations. The second is that it is a career service, which means life time employment. This latter point was a basic principle of the Northcote-Trevelyan Report. The French civil service is divided into sub-groups or corps. Within these corps, the development of expertise and specialisation is very important. The largest such corps is primary school teachers. Others include tax inspectors, magistrates, diplomats and administrators. Most members of the administrative corps are recruited through the Ecole National d'Administration (ENA or National Administrative College). One of the key objectives of this college is "to reform and revitalise recruitment to the senior levels of the French civil service" (Stevens, 1992, p. 125). However, its role is far more extensive, as Stevens (p. 126) points out:

> The ENA serves three main purposes; first it conducts the initial recruitment of potential top civil servants; secondly, through its own testing, examining and ranking processes it selects the members of the different corps and thus marks out those who are destined for truly high-flying careers, and thirdly it provides an initiation into various aspects of administrative life and a measure of work experience and training.

Similar to the British model, ministers are in charge of their departments and the civil servants within them. However, while this is the legal position, the reality is that ministers tend not to get too involved in administrative affairs.

Arguably, this is also fairly similar to the British model. The real difference is that the French civil servants are specialists whereas the traditional British civil servants are generalists – people who can turn their hands to any task. Greater specialisation may actually improve the performance of the British civil service, without the need for politicisation.

The case in favour of politicisation of the civil service

The problem with the constitutional position (that ministers make policy and civil servants implement it) is that it is an idealised perspective. Ministers seek advice from their civil servants. It has to be a matter of trust as to the impartiality of this advice. Rather than there being a healthy working relationship, there are alternative perspectives. The first of these is known as the adversarial model. In effect this model presents a case against the idealised perspective of the formal constitutional model. It is very difficult for ministers to translate the formal authority into real power. Ministers come, ministers go, but the civil servants remain in place. Ministers do not get to see the papers of their predecessors (even if they come from the same political party). There are cabinet reshuffles every two or three years and elections at least every five years. Added to this, it takes at least a year for ministers to get to grips with their portfolios – that is until they start to understand what is going on in the department. During this period, the civil servants effectively 'run' the department. There may be existing "departmental" views on particular policies. These may be foisted upon unsuspecting ministers. Of course, if the minister refuses, the civil servants merely wait for the next incumbent and then try again. Thus in this perspective, there is a constant struggle for power and control between the civil servants and the politicians. Such a perspective was presented in the television series Yes, Minister, where the senior civil servant (Sir Humphrey Appleby) ran rings around the Minister for Administrative Affairs (Jim Hacker). Thus, to prevent such a scenario from occurring, the politicisation of the civil service would reduce the opportunity for intransigent civil servants to manipulate their ministers.

Some of this concern has already been addressed with the increasing use of special advisers by ministers. As noted earlier in this chapter, these special advisers can offer alternative perspectives on policy beyond those of the civil service. In fact, it sometimes appears with the current Labour Government that ministers are more prepared to listen to the advice of their advisers rather than their civil servants. The problem is that there are very few special advisers (numbering less than one hundred) but around half a million civil servants. Even where the special advisers may have the ear of their minister, they may be undermined by the established civil servants.

An example of this was over the resignation of Jo Moore and eventually her minister Stephen Byers. Civil servants in the Department of Transport, Local Government and the Regions complained that Byers was more willing to listen to Jo Moore than to their advice. The relationship between Jo Moore and the civil servants was very poor. Admittedly, Jo Moore was not considered the most tactful of people, especially with her suggestion that in the aftermath of the twin towers tragedy on September 11th, it was "a good time to bury bad news". However, there were allegations of a similar tactic at the time of Princess Margaret's funeral. This allegation turned out to be totally fictitious; one which had been developed and leaked by civil servants within the department. In the investigations after the resignation of Jo Moore, Jonathan Baume (General Secretary of the Association of First Division Civil Servants) described her as a classic textbook bully. This example, although a little extreme, highlights the lengths to which the civil service may go in undermining political appointees. The politicisation of the upper echelons of the civil service may prevent the deterioration of the relationship between the professional administrators and the political appointees. Arguably, the process of politicisation has already begun. Greenwood (2000) highlights this debate by asking "Should the civil service become fully politicised?"

This gradual politicisation of the civil service stems back to the mid-1960s. However, it was during the Thatcher period that the covert politicisation of the civil service commenced. Thatcher wanted like-minded thinkers in the civil service – people who were at the cutting edge of managerialism, who could assist in her radical programme to 'roll back the frontiers of the state'. Prime ministers in the past were theoretically entitled to appoint senior civil service positions, yet Thatcher was the first to 'interfere' in the appointments process, asking "Is he one of us?" Such interference raised the spectre of the civil service being politicised. Again, as with the use of special advisers, it was a painfully slow process. The 'political' appointees did not necessarily receive the same respect within the civil service as others. This was most notable in the sacking of Peter Kemp – who was definitely 'one of us'.

Kemp had been given the job of implementing the Next Steps Programme ("Improving Management in Government: The Next Steps", written by Sir Robin Ibbs, published in February 1988). This was the breaking up of the monolithic civil service into a policy advising core, with executive agencies responsible for policy implementation. Currently there are over one hundred agencies. The agencies worked at arms length from the government, but are still accountable to their parent department. Each agency has a Chief Executive who is appointed through open competition. Most Chief Executives have little experience of Whitehall. Many come from the private sector, bringing with them innovative ideas on how to modernise their agency. Thus within the service delivery aspect of the civil service, there has been a huge impact upon neutrality, permanence and anonymity. Chief Executives do not hold down these jobs for life in the way that traditional civil servants do. They are also the public face of the agencies, and can be expected to address select committees in Parliament, or even the media. Thus the anonymity of traditional civil servants is undermined. The neutrality has also disappeared with many of the early appointments belonging to the 'one of us' doctrine – radical, thinkers who followed Thatcher's idea of rolling back the frontiers of the state. Thus the traditional civil service appears to have been undermined by indirect politicisation. However, this does not mean that the traditional civil service no longer exists. It is still there, having evolved to survive what may be viewed as whimsies that will disappear. The reality is that a more radical approach may be needed modelled on the US system.

The US model uses a combination of career civil servants and political appointees. The career service is based on appointment by merit, permanence and political neutrality (similar to the British system). However, above this is the political service. This comprises around 3 000 people who are specifically appointed by the President, although confirmation is required by the Senate.

> Here selection is not by merit – indeed, many political appointees have no detailed knowledge of the agency they will be heading. There is no security of tenure… and there is no expectation of political neutrality. To complicate matters further, there is nothing to stop the President asking a 'career' civil servant to take up a 'political' position and on 'political' terms. (Hames and Rae, 1996, p. 164)

This means that the top 'political' civil servants are not hamstrung by the necessity of neutrality and even handedness. Nor are they necessarily bogged down in the civil service ethos. They are more able to push through the President's policies, reducing the possibility of having them watered down or delayed (as often happens in Britain). However, such personal devotion to the President and his policies is not actively encouraged. Ronald Reagan had numerous problems in trying to appoint ideologically driven personnel as the Senate were not overly enthusiastic about some of the proposed appointments. Thus while there is clear politicisation in the upper echelons of the civil service, the cult of personality is not encouraged.

Conclusion

The British civil service has traditionally been based upon political neutrality, permanence and anonymity. Over the past quarter of a century, this traditional perspective has come under much pressure. This has been the case especially with the creation of agencies involved in service delivery. The Chief Executives of these agencies are not career civil servants. Often they are appointed from the private sector — the idea being that they can bring in private sector techniques and work habits. To some extent this has indeed undermined the traditional civil service.

On top of this, the current Blair Government, more than any of its predecessors, has used special advisers for policy guidance rather than the civil service. The use of the political dimension ahead of the civil service has led to some conflict between the neutral civil servants and the politically appointed special advisers. The most public example was the relationship between Jo Moore and senior civil servants at the Department of Transport, Local Government and the Regions. However, this example needs to be tempered with the knowledge that this is probably the most problematic example of working relations between civil servants and political advisers.

Yet with arguments of civil service power being able to undermine the politicians, despite the existence of the special advisers, there are calls for the formal politicisation of the British civil service. The special advisers have provided an alternative dimension for policy formulation which has still not been fully utilised. To prevent the potential intransigence of the British civil service hampering policy development, a broader swathe of political appointees may be useful.

The alternative is to look to the continental experience, where increased training and specialisation are encouraged rather than politicisation. Specialist knowledge from a career-minded civil service may actually be more effective than the blunt instrument of politicisation.

Summary of key points

DEFINITION OF THE CIVIL SERVICE

❑ Servants of the Crown who are employed in a civil capacity and are paid for out of moneys voted by Parliament

❑ Currently there are around half a million civil servants

❑ Holders of political offices, members of the armed forces, local government staff, employees of Parliament, of public corporations and of quangos are NOT civil servants

THE CASE AGAINST POLITICISING THE CIVIL SERVICE

❏ Constitutional position of the civil service is that it is politically neutral, impartial and anonymous

❏ Politicians make decisions, civil servants implement them. A change in Government does NOT change this position

❏ Politically impartial advice is available from the civil service. Political advisors offer the party-politicised (biased) advice

❏ Problems of the 'spoils' system in the USA, where there is a politicised civil service

❏ Politicisation may not be equated with improving the civil service

THE CASE FOR POLITICISING THE CIVIL SERVICE

❏ The constitutional position is idealistic

❏ Advice from the civil service may be biased, although not necessarily party-politically biased

❏ Special advisors appear to be replacing the civil service as a source of information for ministers, and they are too few in number to be involved in the implementation of policy

❏ Politicisation of the civil service may prevent the 'blocking' of morecontroversial pieces of legislation

Further Reading

Butcher, T.; "The Civil Service: Structure and Management" in Pyper, R. and Robins, L. (eds.); *United Kingdom Governance* (Macmillan, 2000)

Greenwood, J.; "Should the civil service become fully politicised?" in Robins, L. and Jones, B. (eds.); *Debates in British Politics Today* (Manchester University Press, 2000)

Hames, T. and Rae, N.; *Governing America* (Manchester University Press, 1996)

Stevens, A.; *The Government and Politics of France* (Macmillan, 1992)

Theakston, K.; "Ministers and Civil Servants" in Pyper, R. and Robins, L. (eds.); *United Kingdom Governance* (Macmillan, 2000)

Internet Sites

www.cabinet-office.gov.uk/central/1999/cscode.htm

This is the civil service code. This site details the constitutional framework within which all civil servants must operate.

www.cabinet-office.gov.uk/central/2001/codconspads.htm

The Code of Conduct for Special Advisers

www.cabinet-office.gov.uk/moderngov/index.htm

The Modernising Government homepage

CHAPTER EIGHT

Quangos

INTRODUCTION

The role of quangos (Quasi-Autonomous Non-Governmental Organisations) in British politics is a difficult one to evaluate. Much of the problem is down to an actual definition of the concept. In effect, there is little agreement as to what constitutes a quango. The government has its' own definition, while experts in this area of British politics have a significantly different view. The Government (both the current Blair Government and its' Conservative predecessors) prefer the term Non-Departmental Public Body (NDPB). This term was used by Leon Pliatzky in his report on quangos in 1980. By using the term NDPB, the actual number of bodies included under the label quango is significantly reduced. The government publishes a comprehensive list of these bodies every year in a report entitled Public Bodies. The definition used is:

> A body which has a role in the processes of national government, but is not a government department or part of one, and which accordingly operates to a greater or lesser extent at arm's length from Ministers. (Cabinet Office, 1997, p. 3)

Conversely, Weir and Hall (1994) use the term Extra-Governmental Organisation (EGO). These are defined as: "executive bodies of a semi-autonomous nature which effectively act as agencies for central government and carry out government policies" (Weir and Hall, 1994, p.8). This approach is far wider and includes a range of bodies excluded by Pliatzky and the Government. The differences can be seen in Table 8.1 and Table 8.2

Quango

A Quango (Quasi-Autonomous Non-Governmental Organisation) is an unelected body. Membership is appointed. Quangos operate at arms length from the Government, and implement Government policies.

Table 8.1 Types of Non-Departmental Public Bodies

❏   *Executive bodies* (e.g. Arts Council, Equal Opportunities Commission, Police Complaints Authority)

❏   *Advisory Committees* (e.g. Advisory Committee on Advertising, National Disability Council, Women's National Commission)

❏   *Tribunals* (e.g. Disability Appeals Tribunal, Employment Tribunals, Registered Homes Tribunal)

❏   *Boards of Visitors* (watchdogs of the prison system)

Table 8.2 Bodies included by the EGO approach but excluded from the NDPB approach

❏   NHS bodies, including local trusts

❏   Nationalised Industries (e.g. Scottish Water), Public Corporations (e.g. BBC), and Non-Ministerial Government Departments (e.g. Regulatory Agencies of the privatised utilities, including Ofwat, Ofgas, Oftel

❏   Police authorities

❏   Local Public Spending Bodies (e.g. further and higher education bodies, Grant-maintained schools, local enterprise companies)

It must be noted that in the Governments publication *Public Bodies 2002*, the nationalised industries, public corporations and NHS Trusts are acknowledged as Public Bodies but not included under the label NDPB. In total, as of 31 March 2002, there were 834 public bodies, of which 797 were NDPBs (*Public Bodies 2002*, p. v).

Consequently, different organisations may be included under the label 'quango'. It largely depends upon whether you wish to adopt a narrow approach to the concept or a broader one.

Thus, noting that there is no agreed definition of the term 'quango' beyond the idea of arms length government, it is often easier to examine the general functions of quangos. These can be laid out in a fairly clear manner, although it is important to note that not all quangos carry out the same functions. The different types, as detailed in table 8.1 give an indication as to the different functions of quangos.

In general, quangos perform a role of "government-at-arm's length" – they carry out specific tasks on behalf of the government. These tasks may be of a controversial nature where it is argued that basic party politics ought to be excluded. In these circumstances, a quango may be the most appropriate body; for example the Commission for Racial Equality (CRE). The CRE was established in 1976 to fight racial discrimination and promote racial equality.

It came under the auspices of the Home Office, and is supposed to operate with the support of all political parties, regardless of who is in government.

Quangos may also provide advice and information for government ministers. Research may be carried out by a quango for a particular government department. This advice is more likely to be impartial. Being at arms length from the government should mean that the information does not contain any in-built government biases. This specialist advice or information that is provided may be beyond the ability of the particular government department to obtain for itself.

Some quangos are also involved in service delivery. These bodies cover a wide range of functions across the entire remit of government. The Higher Education Funding Council deals with the wide range of problems in funding higher education. A school which has opted out of LEA control is technically a quango providing a service (education) for its' users (the pupils). Health Trusts are quangos that deliver a number of services in the health sector. Quangos involved in service delivery are often performing a task that used to be directly provided by the government (central, regional or local).

The problems with quangos are linked to the issue of democracy. Quangos are unelected and are often perceived as being unaccountable and unrepresentative of society. There have been many stories reported in the press about party-political appointments to quangos. Regardless of how important a role quangos may perform, there are suggestions that quangos may actually undermine the democratic process – that they are actually undemocratic in nature.

Do Quangos enhance democracy?

The case against quangos enhancing democracy

Quangos are generally considered to be unrepresentative of society. The vast majority of appointments appear to be party-political, or from the world of business. Consequently, various sections of society are not always represented – gender, ethnicity, class, etc. There appears to be an idea that "a safe pair of hands" is needed in each appointment, and this tends to be equated with white, middle class males.

Steps have been taken to address these accusations. The Commissioner for Public Appointments (CPA) was established in 1995. This was a response to the investigations into standards in public life carried out by the Nolan Committee. In establishing such a post, it was hoped that public confidence in quangos and quango appointments might increase. According to the internet homepage of the CPA, the actual task is:

> The Commissioner monitors, regulates, reports and advises on...
> Ministerial appointments to public bodies. Government
> departments are required to follow the Commissioner's Code of
> Practice and detailed Guidance when processing these public
> appointments.
>
> *(www.ocpa.gov.uk/)*

With the opening up of the appointments process, the expectation was that
quango appointments would become more representative of society. While
steps are clearly being taken, the expected transformation is moving very
slowly. According to the 2001/2002 Annual Report of the CPA, out of around
3500 appointments, 39% were women (compared to 33% in 1999). The
government has a target here of 50% by 2005. Ethnic minority appointments
comprised less than 9% of the total (compared to less than 5% in 1999).
Nearly 3% of those appointed to quangos declared a disability
(*www.ocpa.gov.uk/reports/ocpa07.pdf*).

Another complaint about quangos is that they appear to be unaccountable.
While many structures exist to hold the various tiers of government to
account, quangos appear to be excluded. For example, while all quangos are
obliged to produce an annual report, there may be no obligation to hold any
public meetings or produce minutes of meetings for the public. According to
Public Bodies 2002 (p. 74), the Police Complaints Authority held no public
meetings, offered no public minutes, and did not publish a register of public
interests. The Parole Board, on the other hand, offered public minutes and had
a register of public interests, but did not hold any public meetings. Added to
this, very few quangos are inspected by the ombudsman (who investigates
maladministration), although the CPA does investigate complaints about
quango appointments. In 2001/2002, the CPA investigated 38 complaints
(compared to 5 in 1997/98). A further 83 were referred to the appropriate
department by the CPA (compared to 39 in 1997/98). Only 50% of all
complaints received about appointments were actually investigated (source:
www.ocpa.gov.uk/reports/ocpa07.pdf).

Yet where the unaccountability is most clearly perceived is in the area of
finance. In 2001/2002, Executive NDPBs spent just under £21 billion (*Public
Bodies 2002*, p. x). Of this, over £15 billion was funded directly by the
government. However, this applies only to Executive NDPBs. Even using
Table 8.1, this excludes Advisory NDPBs, Tribunals and Boards of Visitors. In
2001/2002, there were 192 Executive NDPBs (*Public Bodies 2002*). There are
over 600 other bodies (from those which would be included in Table 8.1),
before including Nationalised Industries, opted-out schools, NHS Trusts, etc.
The Correctional Service Accreditation Panel (which is an Advisory NDPB

under the Home Office which looks into the work of the Prison and Probation Services with regard to reducing re-offending) was funded by the Government to the amount of £269 000.00 (*Public Bodies 2002*, p. 75). The Criminal Injuries Compensation Appeals Panel is a Tribunal NDPB with the Home Office. Its' government funding was over £5 million (*Public Bodies 2002*, p. 77). Thus the £21 billion spent by the Executive NDPBs is not the full amount spent by NDPBs or other quangos. According to Flinders and Smith (1999), EGO spending in the mid-1990s was somewhere in the vicinity of £60 billion. This was approximately one third of all government spending at that time.

In the consultation paper "Opening Up Quangos" (1997), the government appeared to recognise the apparent lack of accountability. It stated that "there is no obvious mechanism by which quangos can be held to account for their activity" (p.6). Since then, some attempts have been made to change this situation. The CPA can investigate appointments. The Comptroller and Auditor General can inspect the finances of all Executive NDPBs. The audit arrangements for other quangos are not so open. According to *Public Bodies 2002*, only Executive NDPBs in the Home Office were audited. No audit information was provided for any other NDPB within this government department, even though the Home Office spent over £2.5 million and the Government spent almost £6 million on these bodies.

Ultimately, quangos have been described as being undemocratic. The simple reason for this is that members are appointed rather than elected. A key feature of any democratic system is open and free elections. With regard to the quango state in Britain, there appears to be a democratic deficit. By this, it means that there is simply a lack of direct democratic control over quangos. There may be indirect democratic control via central government, in that the parent department can be held responsible for the actions of the quangos within its remit. Yet it is very difficult to hold central government to account for what may be a localised problem. It may not even be appropriate to hold a government minister to account for the actions of a group of appointed people – even if the minister appointed them. If the minister is to be held to account for the actions of a quango, then perhaps the ministers department ought to be carrying out the work of the quango rather than providing the quango with some degree of autonomy.

The secrecy of quangos makes the situation even worse. Under previous governments, quango membership was concealed. This situation has been remedied to some degree in that the CPA monitors quango appointments. However, in many cases, there is still a high degree of secrecy, with limited information being divulged to the public about the actions and the spending of quangos. While the CPA may ensure a level of openness with regard to appointments, the democratic accountability remains indirect at best. It is still very difficult to hold quango members to account for their actions and their spending.

The case for quangos enhancing democracy

To some extent, the case for quangos enhancing democracy overlaps with the functions of quangos which were outlined in the introduction to this chapter. However, it is useful to reiterate some of these points to emphasize the important role played by quangos.

The primary function of many quangos is as a source of information. Quangos can provide impartial expert advice to the government. This could be on very sensitive issues such as BSE or GM crops. Added to this, quangos can provide a rapid response to matters of concern. The Nolan Committee was established in 1994 to investigate sleaze in public life, and to define acceptable standards of conduct for those who work in this area. The CPA, which was proposed by the Nolan Committee, monitors quango membership. This is to assist in ensuring the impartiality of the advice given by quangos.

An important aspect of the advice from quangos is its impartiality. An alternative way of examining this advice is that it is 'depoliticised'. As noted earlier in this chapter, there are some aspects of government that are better addressed beyond the party-political sphere. Political considerations may need to be dropped in the hope of achieving a sensible outcome to a particular problem. Issues as diverse as race relations, health and safety, and higher education funding are all likely to benefit from depoliticisation.

This depoliticisation is also emphasised through the phrase 'arm's length government'. Although quangos are government appointed (following the CPA guidelines), they are supposed to operate at a distance from the government. There should be no government interference in the activities of a quango, in the same way as there should be no government interference in quango appointments. This clearly assists in the depoliticisation not just of the quangos but specifically their activities.

A link to both depoliticisation and expert advice is the idea that quangos can be used to improve service delivery. Being at arm's length from the government enables a quango to concentrate specifically upon the task in hand. This is not too dissimilar to the way in which agencies function as part of the civil service. Quangos are single-purpose bodies. They are able to specialise and develop new and more efficient practices, in a way that other bodies (such as local government or central government) can not. Quangos are unencumbered by pressures from which multi-purpose service deliverers often suffer. Although the policies may be derived from the government, the actual implementation of the policies is left to the quangos. Thus the quangos can develop their expertise, which in turn can be used by the government to adapt their policies. The quangos then respond by improving their service delivery.

All of this actually addresses the democratic deficit. At first, such an idea may not seem obvious. Quangos are unelected which is equated with being undemocratic. Yet, although unelected, quangos can still improve democracy. At the most basic level, democracy is improved via accountability. Quangos are ultimately accountable to their parent department, and thus to the Minister. The Minister, in turn, is accountable to Parliament and, ultimately, to the public.

More importantly, the public are empowered as consumers of public services. It does not really matter who provides the service as long as it is responsive to the needs and demands of the users. This particular line of argument was developed by William Waldegrave when he was a member of John Major's Cabinet in the early 1990s. If you are dissatisfied with a particular product, then you purchase an alternative. The same ought to apply to services. If the quality of service being delivered is not up to scratch, then you should be able to change service provider. When services are provided by the local authority, you can lobby your local council to improve a given service. However, councils have a reputation for being exceedingly slow to react to any problems. This leaves the options of voting your council out of office at the next election, or to move house. The former option is very difficult. It is very difficult to vote a party out of office. An average turnout of below 40% for local government elections highlights the extent of disinterest in local politics. It may actually be the case that the voting public is dissatisfied with local government processes, and does not believe that anything can be done about it via the ballot box. Democracy through the ballot box does not always appear to work.

Thus quangos may actually empower people. They are considered to be far more responsive to public demands because the public, as consumers of a service, demand the best possible service. If the public are not satisfied, they are likely to change service provider. Ultimately, democracy is also improved as accountability is increased. Quangos, as service providers, must operate in the best interests of the consumers. If the consumers are dissatisfied, they have the opportunity to change service provider.

One small footnote here is that in the case of a monopoly service provider, there is no alternative. A lack of alternative in service provision may leave the consumer in the same position as with former council provision – an inability to obtain change.

Conclusion

Quangos, NDPBs, EGOs, or whatever term is used, are a complicated part of British politics. They have become an essential part of British politics as well. Steps have been taken by the current Government in acknowledging those public bodies that do not fit the definition of NDPB. Yet it is still the case that not all public bodies are included. It is unclear as to how the Government accounts for those organisations that do not fit its' definition.

Quangos may appear undemocratic because they are unelected and secretive, and appear unaccountable and unrepresentative of society. Yet, at the same time, they perform a valuable role in service delivery, in the depoliticisation of sensitive issues, and in providing impartial expert information for the Government. The creation of bodies such as the CPA has started to open up the world of quangos to public scrutiny. However, as noted before, it has been an exceedingly slow process. It is always interesting to listen to politicians on the subject of quangos. When in Opposition, quangos are condemned; yet when in Government, quangos are still used extensively.

Summary of key points

DEFINITION OF QUANGO

- ❏ Quasi-Autonomous Non-Governmental Organisation
- ❑ Unelected body which operates at arms length from the Government
- ❏ Key functions include implementing Government policies

THE CASE AGAINST QUANGOS ENHANCING DEMOCRACY

- ❏ Selected not elected membership
- ❏ Limited accountability
- ❏ A high degree of secrecy surrounds the operations of many quangos

THE CASE FOR QUANGOS ENHANCING DEMOCRACY

- ❏ Source of impartial, expert information
- ❏ Depoliticisation of divisive issues (Government-at arms-length)
- ❏ Unelected does not mean unaccountable

Further Reading

Cabinet Office; "Opening Up Quangos: A Consultation Paper" (1997)

Flinders, M. and Smith, M. (eds.); *Quangos, Accountability and Reform: The Politics of Quasi-Government* (Macmillan, 1999)

Greenwood, J., Pyper, R. and Wilson, D.; *New Public Administration in Britain* (Routledge, 2002, 3rd edition) (esp. chapter 8)

Skelcher, C.; *The Appointed State: Quasi-governmental Organizations and Democracy* (Open University Press, 1998)

Stott, T.; "Quangos: are they unloved and misunderstood?" in Robins, L. and Jones, B. (eds.); *Debates in British Politics Today* (Manchester University Press, 2000)

Weir, S. and Hall, W.; *Ego-Trip: Extra-governmental organisation in the United Kingdom and their accountability* (The Charter88 Trust, 1994)

Internet Sites

www.cabinet-office.gov.uk/agencies-publicbodies

The Cabinet Office website on quangos and public bodies

www.ocpa.gov.uk

Home page of the Office of the Commissioner for Public Appointments. This body is independent of the Cabinet Office, and advises on appointments to public bodies

www.publicappointments.gov.uk

The Public Appointments Unit

CHAPTER NINE
Pressure Groups

INTRODUCTION

Pressure groups have played a role in British Politics for many years. Even in the eighteenth and nineteenth centuries, pressure groups such as the Anti-Slavery Society, the Chartists and the Anti-Corn Law League played an active role in politics. During the twentieth century, and in particular after World War Two, there was a huge expansion in the number of pressure groups operating within the British political system. In the British Directory of Associations (as cited in Baggott, 1995, p. 1) around 7000 pressure groups are listed. This list includes bodies as diverse as the Simplified Spelling Society and the Confederation of British Industry.

Yet despite the large number of groups that function within the British political system, the formal constitutional approach to democracy in Britain places a heavy emphasis upon Parliament. There is no formal recognition of pressure groups. Even Ivor Jennings in his book *The Law and the Constitution* (1959) ignored such group interests – presumably because they did not fit into the formal structures of government.

> ### Pressure group
>
> An organisation with a shared interest, cause or concern which attempts to influence the government, another organisation and/or the public with respect to that interest, cause or concern. Pressure groups seek access to the decision makers, and attempt to influence them.

Pressure groups seek influence, either directly or indirectly. It may be over a particular government policy, or over public opinion. They do not seek to challenge the government, in that pressure groups do not seek to become the government. Rather, they complement government. Any definition of the concept pressure group will highlight these ideas – that pressure groups wish to have influence. More specifically, these groups wish to influence policy over a very narrow range of concerns – possibly even a single issue. Thus

Greenpeace is concerned with environmental issues; trades unions are concerned with the well-being of their members; anti-road campaigners are trying to prevent new road-building schemes.

In sum, a pressure group is an organisation of people with a specific interest or concern. They may attempt to influence either the government or the public with regard to that interest or concern. Pressure groups do not wish to form part of the government, they may simply wish access to, and influence over, the decision makers. Such themes as these are evident in most definitions of the concept pressure group.

Thus pressure groups are seen as a useful tool in promoting democratic ideals. It is far easier for a single group to be heard on a given issue rather than individual voices. However, not all pressure groups are equal. They do not all have the same opportunities of access to the decision makers. In fact, some pressure groups attempt to co-opt former politicians into their organisations in the hope of improving access to the decision makers. Wealthier organisations are able to fund expensive campaigns to promote their particular perspective on a given issue or concern. This means that there is not a level playing field for the operation of pressure groups. In fact it may be that the bigger, better financed organisations have a far better opportunity to influence decision makers. This may be to the detriment of democracy in Britain.

Do pressure groups undermine democracy?
The case for pressure groups undermining democracy

One charge against pressure groups is that they undermine Parliamentary democracy. Pressure groups often pursue extra-Parliamentary methods by working closely with ministers and civil servants. This gives them the opportunity to have an input in the formulation of legislation prior to it going before Parliament. This is denied to MPs, who merely get to comment and debate on the legislation when it is presented to the House. In this way, Parliament may be seen as no more than a body which legitimises the decisions taken by the Executive (see Chapter Five for more details). These decisions may well have been strongly influenced by pressure groups. It is exceedingly difficult to find out the extent of pressure group involvement in the formulation of legislation due to the secretive nature of proceedings. This point is examined later in this chapter.

However, what we see here is the possible interference with one of the underpinnings of the British constitution – parliamentary sovereignty. As already examined in Chapter Three, the influence of the executive over the legislative powers of Parliament is such that Parliament merely rubber stamps the decisions proposed by the executive. Pressure groups, with access to the decision makers may actually exacerbate this situation, placing further emphasis upon the executive and far less upon the role of Parliament.

A further point to note about the undermining of Parliament is that MPs can be held to account to the electorate at election time for their actions. Thus MPs have to defend themselves publicly. Pressure groups, on the other hand, do not appear to be accountable to anybody – except possibly their own membership. The advice that they give will most probably benefit their own membership or possibly only sections of it, but not necessarily anyone else. Thus pressure groups can be seen as narrow self-interested organisations out to further their own particular cause.

Added to this, pressure groups are often accused of not being truly representative of the mass of their membership, less say all of public opinion. This tends to apply in particular to the large powerful groups such as the trades unions and the Confederation of British Industry, but also to bodies such as the RSPCA and the Countryside Alliance (on issues such as fox hunting). These groups are not accountable to the public and are often perceived as merely pursuing their own narrow aims – or more specifically, those of the leadership - rather than looking at a wider context.

So, not only are pressure groups unrepresentative, but they can also be accused of narrow self-interest. One of the features of pressure groups is that they are single-issue organisations. This tends to be a part of any definition of the term pressure group. However, the problem is that these self-interest tendencies may obscure the greater picture. A recent example of such self-interest was evident in the fuel protests in September 2000. Lorry drivers and farmers forced the entire country to a standstill by blockading fuel depots and preventing fuel being delivered. Their concern was the high levels of taxation on fuel. They demanded that British prices be reduced to those seen in France. However lorry drivers ignored the range of other duties that French lorry drivers have to pay: notably motorway taxes, but also the much higher levels of direct taxation experienced, not just in France but throughout most of the continent. Similarly, the farmers failed to point out that "red" diesel which is used on farms only has around three pence duty compared to almost 50 pence duty paid on normal diesel in 1999. Admittedly farmers are not permitted to use red diesel outside of their farm land but the fact of the matter is that they pay reduced duties for their product.

Despite all of these details, a combination of the narrow-mindedness of the protestors and the frenzy whipped up by the media almost resulted in Britain grinding to a halt. Emergency services could not function properly. In rural areas many children could not even get to school. All of this was a result of the demand for cheap fuel.

To the list of self-interest, unrepresentativeness and the undermining of Parliamentary democracy, it is also possible to highlight the power of the bigger pressure groups. It is the big battalions who have all of the advantages in the matters of propaganda, wealth and publicity. It tends to follow that the stronger a group is in terms of riches and contacts, the more likely it is to achieve its goals. This tends to apply to groups linked with big business. The weaker consumer group interests like those dealing with children, the elderly or the disabled, to name but a few, because of their relative poverty and weak organisation tend to lose out to the big battalions. Compare the power and influence of an organisation such as the Campaign for Real Ale (CAMERA) which is after a better quality product, with those of the big breweries. In a straight fight between the two to influence the government, it is the latter that tends to win.

A final point about the way in which pressure groups undermine democracy is to do with secrecy. One of the major faults in government *per se* is an obsession with secrecy, both in negotiations and consultations, as well as the disclosure of information. Pressure groups appear to be quite happy to collude. It was no wonder that Finer entitled his book on pressure groups *Anonymous Empire* (1966, 2nd edition) and little has changed. Most pressure groups do not operate in full public view, except if publicity is needed to combat an opponent's view. At the same time, civil servants will only have dealings with pressure groups if secrecy is preserved. While governments may talk about openness, the reality is that there is little information as to which groups have been consulted, or what advice they have given. In the Budget, when taxes are increased on alcohol or tobacco, there is normally little or no outcry from the brewers or the tobacco companies. These increases make their products more expensive and potentially less desirable to the public, yet there are no complaints. When fuel duties go up, the outcry is huge from the Road Hauliers Association and other motoring organisations – an extreme form of which occurred in September 2000, as was noted earlier in this chapter.

In sum, the public is unaware as to the extent of pressure group influence in policy making. Most groups are unrepresentative of society, are secretive, and have very narrow self-interests. Secrecy, in particular, undermines the democratic process. Pressure groups, and especially the larger ones, appear happy to collude in such a system.

The case against pressure groups undermining democracy

A key role for pressure groups is that they provide extra opportunities for participation in politics. Voting, which is the main form of participation for the majority of the British people, occurs once every five years for Parliamentary elections and elections to the European Parliament, while local government elections are held every four years (as are elections to the Scottish Parliament, Welsh Assembly and Northern Ireland Assembly). Participation in pressure group activity broadens these opportunities. Rather than simply placing a mark next to a candidate or party, pressure group activity enables people to actually participate in the decision making process. This could be via direct meetings with a councillor, an MP, a minister or civil servants. Alternatively, it could mean co-ordinating petition signings, or organising a rally or a public meeting – as well as participating in any of these. There is some form of interaction in each case, as opposed merely to marking a piece of paper. The participation in pressure groups also enables longer-term involvement in the decision making process rather than a five minute trip to a polling station.

Added to this, participation in pressure group activity enables a particular issue to be highlighted. Political parties are more concerned about the broader sweep of policies. Pressure groups enable specialisation. Two examples of different approaches have been seen in recent years. The first was the Snowdrop Campaign. In March 1996, a gunman killed sixteen schoolchildren and their teacher in Dunblane. After this tragedy, a campaign was launched to ban the private ownership of handguns. This was a high profile campaign which gained support from the bereaved parents as well as the general public. Despite the best efforts of the pro-gun lobby, a ban was eventually introduced.

More recently there was the national protest against the war with Iraq. Over a million and a half people marched in London, with a smaller march in Glasgow in February 2003 to protest about the US and UK warmongering. It was not that these people necessarily supported Saddam Hussein but rather they objected to the way in which the British and US Governments were effectively trying to invade Iraq without a United Nations mandate. Other protests were carried out throughout the UK at other times, even by school children. The protests were not confined to Britain either – they were global, with marches throughout the USA, Australia, New Zealand, Japan and many other countries. Despite this, the British and US Governments ignored global opinion and pursued their militaristic policies. The important thing to note here is that not all pressure groups are successful, despite the vast numbers that may support them.

Another important aspect of the role of pressure groups in enhancing democracy is the way on which they can protect minority interests. These interests are often overlooked by the major political parties. Therefore it is only through banding together that individuals with so-called minority interests can hope to have their views represented and expressed. Examples of such organisations include Age Concern (catering for the elderly), Shelter (homelessness), and MIND (mental health sufferers). While each of these minority groups may get support from the government, most of this support is due to the actions of the pressure groups which work on behalf of their interests. The reality is that political parties see very few votes in supporting such minority interests. Even ideas such as mobilising the 'grey vote' gains little support with political parties. The pressure groups have to lobby and cajole the government to help the lot of their members.

Indirectly linked to minority interests is another role for pressure groups which enhances democracy. They are often critics of the government, and may be involved in scrutinising the government and holding it to account. The enthusiasm and commitment of many pressure groups is such that they can often scrutinise the actions of the government far more effectively than political parties operating in Westminster. British democracy is not so perfect that governments cannot endure checks beyond those offered by opposing MPs. Pressure groups can present important, detailed information that can influence government policy. Thus in 1995 Greenpeace were able to persuade the Shell Oil Company and the British Government (who supported Shell's proposals) not to dispose of the Brent Spar oil rig by dumping it in the mid-Atlantic but rather to dismantle the rig instead – the adverse effects on the environment would be far less if the rig were not to be dumped. (It must be noted here that the information from Greenpeace on this particular issue, like that of both Shell and the Government, was not wholly accurate). Shell and the British Government originally ignored the Greenpeace alternative, and it was only through extensive lobbying across Europe, and particularly in Germany (where some Shell petrol stations were damaged) that the decision was reversed. The Brent Spar was towed to a Norwegian fjord, where it was decommissioned and recycled as a foundation for a new ferry terminal in Mekjarvik, Norway.

Although we are noting criticism here, it is also important to acknowledge that criticism can also be constructive, and can even involve praise for Government actions. The Snowdrop Campaign, for example, commended the Government on its prompt action to ban handguns.

A theoretical justification can also be made for the need and desirability of pressure groups. Fundamental freedoms, many of which are supposedly protected under the Human Rights Act of 1998 (see Chapter Four) such as speech, association, and religious practice, can be furthered by pressure group action. While the law is supposed to protect the people, it is often through pressure group actions that people actually become aware of their rights. Governments may also become aware of strong feelings that may be generated by campaigns and ignore them at their peril. This has been evident in the campaigns both in favour and against fox hunting. After the marches against the possible war in Iraq in February 2003, Tony Blair, it is alleged, actually started to prepare his resignation if the war was to go badly. This shows the extent of influence wielded by public opinion but also the stubbornness of politicians. If Blair was that aware of the strength of public opinion, the rhetorical question is why did he persist with the policy?

Pressure group action does not always succeed. The important thing in a democracy is that people have the opportunity to express their concerns and feelings. They may not always be able to influence the decision makers but a lack of protest (or support) might leave the decision makers with the perspective of a total lack of opposition to their policies. Thus pressure groups do enhance democracy.

Conclusion

Pressure group activity is on the increase. The number of people who were mobilised to protest about the war with Iraq – not just in Britain, but globally – was phenomenal. There was an apparent feeling that the politicians were unable to prevent Tony Blair from taking Britain into an apparently illegal war. The phrase was simple: "Not in my name". However, the protests failed in that the war was fought. Yet there was a backlash, and it was seen to some degree in the local, Scottish Parliamentary and Welsh Assembly elections of May 2003, and in the local and European Parliamentary elections in 2004. The turnout in most cases (especially in 2003) was abysmal. It appeared that the voting public had become even more disillusioned about politicians than ever before – in the most basic of terms that they do not listen to the public.

Yet with this mobilisation of public opinion, across all age groups, there is an obvious interest in politics. Voting is perceived to be inconsequential. Alternative action beckons. The question to ask is whether or not this is democratic. The undermining of Parliament is suggested, but conversely it could be argued that Blair undermined Parliament by forcing a three-line whip on the votes on Iraq rather than having a vote of conscience. Democracy is actually alive and well, and pressure groups can help. They have their flaws: they are secretive, unelected, and not obviously accountable to anyone. Yet they give an opportunity for the people to at least express their opinions. That, at least, is a sign of an open democratic system.

Summary of key points

DEFINITION OF PRESSURE GROUP

❑ An organisation with a shared interest or concern

❑ It attempts to influence the decision makers

❑ They want access to the decision making process

THE CASE FOR PRESSURE GROUPS UNDERMINING DEMOCRACY

❑ Pressure groups are unelected and are also unaccountable

❑ They undermine Parliament by gaining access to the civil service or to ministers during the drafting of legislative proposals which then go before Parliament

❑ Pressure groups tend to be unrepresentative of society

❑ Focus on narrow self-interest

❑ Pressure groups are often very secretive

THE CASE AGAINST PRESSURE GROUPS UNDERMINING DEMOCRACY

❑ Pressure groups provide extra opportunities for participation

❑ They can specialise on their specific issue or concern

❑ They are able to criticise the government or other organisations

❑ Pressure groups can protect minority concerns

Further Reading

Baggott, R.; *Pressure Groups Today* (Manchester University Press, 1995)

Baggott, R.; *Pressure Groups and the Policy Process* (Sheffield Hallam University Press, 2000)

Finer, S.; *Anonymous Empire: a study of the lobby in Great Britain* (Pall Mall Press, 1966, 2nd edition)

Grant, W.; *Pressure Groups and British Politics* (Macmillan, 2000)

Jennings, I.; *The Law and the Constitution* (University of London Press, 1959, 5th edition)

Kelly, R. and Foster, S.; "Acting on Impulse? Instinct, Interest and Support in British Politics" *Talking Politics* vol. 15, 2003

Internet sites

*www.governmentguide.co.uk/netguide/PPF/UK_Government_Guide/Pressure_Gro
ups/GCID/1370/Guide.asp*

This is a guide to pressure groups which operate within the UK, giving web
addresses and comment about the organisations listed

www.historylearningsite.co.uk/pressure_groups.htm

This website gives clear definitions and different categorisations of pressure
groups, as well as asking the question as to whether they add to or detract from
democracy

www.politicsbrief.co.uk/Main%20List%20of%20pressure%20groups.htm

This site gives a list of pressure groups under different categories e.g.
constitutional reform, Europe, etc.

CHAPTER TEN
Political Parties

INTRODUCTION

Political parties have become a key feature of British politics. Almost all reports on British elections focus upon the success or failure of the parties. Even when independent candidates win election, it is portrayed as a defeat for a specific party. Thus in the 1997 General Election, the constituency of Tatton was lost by the Conservatives to an Independent candidate. In 2001, Wyre Forest was lost by Labour to an Independent candidate. Even in the 2003 local government elections, Labour lost control of Mansfield Council to the Independents. Thus the independent candidates are clearly portrayed as the exception. It is normally the political parties who are the focus of attention.

Political Party

An organisation of broadly like-minded people who work together to gain electoral office. A political party tends to be underpinned by an ideology – a system of ideas, assumptions and values – that can be used to explain issues or policies

When examining British politics in general terms, the focus tends to be upon Parliament, and specifically the House of Commons. It is in this arena, as with devolved and local politics, where parties predominate. In the previous chapter, the subject under discussion was pressure groups. Pressure groups seek influence – they wish to have influence over the decision makers. Political parties, on the other hand, strive to become the decision makers by fighting elections in an attempt to win office. Rather than having a single issue (as in the case of pressure groups), political parties cover a wide range of issues. These areas, and the policies that the parties wish to implement upon obtaining office, are presented to the electorate in the form of a party manifesto. Prior to each election, political parties normally issue their manifestos. The expectation is that these will become policies and laws prior to the subsequent election. Thus, pressure groups are involved in interest articulation – the voicing of particular concerns, whereas political parties are involved in interest aggregation – various 'interests' are pooled together to form the manifesto.

As a consequence, political parties are sometimes described as 'umbrella' organisations. This is because a wide range of interests are covered by political parties. The Labour Party, for example, includes a large number of trades unions, as well as socialist organisations (such as the Fabian Society), and also some business leaders (such as Bernie Ecclestone). Even the MPs themselves cover a wide perspective, from the likes of Peter Mandelson to Dennis Skinner, from Bob Marshall-Andrews to Jack Straw. The Conservatives and the Liberal Democrats, as well as all the other parties in the UK follow a not too dissimilar pattern.

Having obtained office, a party then provides the government ministers to administer the various departments. This is more easily done when only one party holds power. It is commonly perceived to be far easier to co-ordinate policy through the shared interests of a single party (even though that collection of individuals is in itself a broad coalition of interests) rather than sharing power in coalition with another party. At the same time, the losing parties continue to offer their policy alternatives – the idea of a 'government-in-waiting'.

Political parties are also effective vehicles in keeping government to account. Opposition party members get the opportunity to question Government Ministers and the Prime Minister, as do Government MPs. They also get to assist in the scrutiny of legislation (see Chapter Five for more detail). Yet the ultimate form of accountability is a General Election. It is much easier for accountability to be realised when there is a single party in power who can be 'blamed' for any policy failures. If the errors are great enough then that party will be voted from Office – and in the case of the 1997 General Election, it was a resounding defeat for the Conservative Party.

However, herein there lies a problem. Parliament is based around parties. There is Her Majesty's Loyal Government and Her Majesty's Loyal Opposition. This suggests that there are only two prominent parties. Yet three have already been mentioned in this introduction alone, and the existence of others at least acknowledged. Everything to do with Parliament and elections focuses upon the gains and losses for the Government and the Opposition. Traditional textbooks portray Britain as a two-party system. There are only two mighty parties competing for Office; two broad coalitions covering the swathe of British politics. This suggests that the other parties are, at best, inconsequential, or, at worst, mere figments of our imagination.

Does Britain still have a two-party system?

The case for Britain still having a two-party system

As already noted, the British Parliament appears to be structured around two parties fighting for Office. There is the Government and the Opposition. It suggests only two parties. The current leader of the Government is the Prime Minister – Tony Blair. The current Leader of the Opposition is Michael Howard. Thus the perception that is presented is of two monolithic blocs of MPs in an endless confrontation for power and control. There may be other parties represented in Parliament, but these are largely inconsequential. The role of the Opposition in Parliament is to present itself as an alternative to the Government – a Government-in-waiting. Thus they highlight the mistakes of the Government and present alternative policy proposals.

The structure of Parliamentary proceedings is also based around a two-party system. In Prime Ministers Question Time, or any Ministerial Question Time, there is an alternation of questions between the Government and the Opposition. Thus the Opposition can mount a concerted attack on the Government's record in a given policy area. However, this is undermined by having to 'share' the Opposition questions with the smaller parties. The system is not geared towards multi-party politics. It is a straight fight between the Government and the Opposition, regardless as to the effectiveness of the Opposition party.

In examining the history of Parliament since the formation of modern political parties, the vast bulk of the history has seen only two parties being in a position to hold the reins of power. It has only been in the inter-war period and during the Second World War where the two-party system has been under threat. This was most noticeable during the Great Depression and the duration of the war. The inter-war period was also the time of the demise of the Liberal Party as a political force, and the rise of the Labour Party. Prior to the formation of the Labour Party in the early 1900s, Britain had been a two-party system. From 1867, with the Second Reform Act which extended voting rights, the development of modern political parties can be seen. The loose coalitions of Whigs and Tories evolved into more coherent organisations, taking on the labels Liberal and Conservative. There was a clear alternation of governments: Whigs and Tories, Liberals and Conservatives, dating back to as early as 1832.

Post-World War Two in particular has seen every election being a contest between Labour and the Conservatives. Table 10.1 highlights this very clearly. In every post-war election, the same two parties have dominated electoral proceedings. Between 1950 and 1970, in any single election the Conservatives and Labour collectively failed to win no more than 14 seats (1966 election). Even with the rise of the Liberal Democrats over the last three elections, little has changed. The Liberal Democrats, in their best performance, have won just over 9% of Parliamentary seats (2005 election). The 62 seats won by the Liberal Democrats is less than a third of those won by the Conservatives in the same election – and that was the second worst performance, in terms of seats won, by either of the major parties in the post-war era.

Table 10.1 Seats won in Post-World War Two General Elections

Year	Conservative	Labour	Liberal*	Others**
1945	213	393	12	22
1950	298	315	9	3
1951	321	295	6	3
1955	344	277	6	3
1959	365	258	6	1
1964	304	317	9	0
1966	253	363	12	2
1970	330	287	6	7
Feb. 1974	297	301	14	23
Oct. 1974	277	319	13	26
1979	339	269	11	16
1983	397	209	23	21
1987	376	229	22	23
1992	336	271	20	24
1997	165	419	46	29
2001	166	413	52	28
2005	197	356	62	30

*   In 1983 and 1987, Liberal figures cover the results for the Liberal/SDP Alliance. The figures for 1992 onwards are for the Liberal Democrats.

*   "Others" includes Northern Ireland MPs from Feb. 1974 onwards.

The electoral system is engineered for a straight choice of government. Under the Simple Plurality electoral system, voters are in effect choosing which party they would like to form the government. The idea is to have a strong Executive which can get its' manifesto pledges through Parliament. In the post–war period, on only one occasion (February 1974) has the election result failed to give an outright majority for one political party (see Table 10.2 for full details of post–war government majorities). Admittedly, Government majorities in the post–war period (except February 1974) have ranged between 177 (Labour, 1997) and 3 (Labour, October 1974). The size of the government majorities tends to be a result of the relative closeness between the two major parties rather than the number of seats won by third and minor parties. In the two closest election results, the number of seats not won by the two main parties were 37 (February 1974, with a minority government) and 39 (October 1974, Government majority of 3). The two best results for third and minor parties were in 2001 (winning 80 seats) and 2005 (winning 92).

Table 10.2 *Government majorities in post-war elections*

Year	Governing Party	Majority
1945	Labour	146
1950	Labour	5
1951	Conservative	17
1955	Conservative	58
1959	Conservative	100
1964	Labour	4
1966	Labour	96
1970	Conservative	30
February 1974	Labour (minority)	-33
October 1974	Labour	3
1979	Conservative	43
1983	Conservative	144
1987	Conservative	101
1992	Conservative	21
1997	Labour	177
2001	Labour	165
2005	Labour	67

Britain clearly has a two–party system. The structure of Parliament is geared towards only two parties. The objective of British elections is to choose a government. A strong government that can implement its manifesto proposals has been the hallmark of British Government. Only two parties have a viable opportunity of winning an election – the Conservatives and Labour. With the exceptions of part of the inter-war period and World War Two, the history of British Parliamentary Government has been two parties vying for power. It must also be noted that during the Second World War, elections were suspended until 1945. Thus the wartime coalition was not a result of an election (the previous one being held in 1935) but rather a response to the war – a desire for national unity in the face of adversity.

The case against Britain still having a two-party system

The argument that Britain has a two-party system, for the most part, rests upon the number of seats won in Parliament. In particular, the period 1950–1970 when the Conservative and Labour won most seats and most votes. However, this small period of history is more of an exception than a reality. The fewest number of parties gaining representation in a post-war Parliament has been three, and that occurred in 1964. After the 2001 General Election, nine parties had representation in Parliament, as well as one Independent MP. In examining Table 10.1, the label "Others" actually covers a large number of political parties. A list of the parties under this label is presented in Table 10.3

Thus what can be drawn from this table is that a wide range of parties have gained election to the British Parliament. Note that Northern Ireland parties are only sitting from the 1974 elections. The Ulster Unionists were effectively part of the Conservative Party. It was only from 1972 that Northern Ireland was governed from Westminster and that all Northern Ireland parties separated themselves from their mainland counterparts.

What is important to note is that some governments have been dependent upon the support of smaller parties to maintain their position in Office. Between 1976 and 1978, the Labour Government formed a pact with the Liberals to stay in power. This was not a formal coalition as the Liberals did not gain any posts in the Cabinet. However, they supported the Labour Party in the House of Commons. Similarly, in the latter days of John Major's Government, the Conservatives were kept in power by the support of the Ulster Unionists in the Commons. Again, there was no formal coalition although the Conservatives did appear to adopt a number of policy stances on Northern Ireland that were in line with the Ulster Unionists.

Table 10.3 Minor Party representation in Post-War Parliaments (number of MPs)

Year	Parties (number of MPs)
1945	Commonwealth Party (1), Communist Party (2), Independent (14), Independent Labour Party (3), Irish Nationalist (2)
1950	Independent (Speaker) (1), Irish Nationalist (2)
1951	Independent (Speaker) (1), Irish Nationalist (2)
1955	Independent (Speaker) (1), Sinn Fein (2)
1959	Independent (Speaker) (1)
1964	-
1966	Independent (Speaker) (1), Republican Labour (1)
1970	Independent (Speaker) (1), Independent Labour (1), Independent Unity (1),Protestant Unionist (1), Republican Labour (1), Scottish Nationalist Party (1), Unity (1)
February 1974	Independent Labour (1), Independent Republican (1), Plaid Cymru (2), Scottish Nationalist Party (7), Social Democratic and Labour Party (1), Ulster Democratic Unionist Party (1), Ulster Unionist Party (7),Vanguard Unionist Progressive Party (3)
October 1974	Independent Republican (1), Plaid Cymru (3), Scottish Nationalist Party (11), Social Democratic and Labour Party (1), Ulster Democratic Unionist Party (1), Ulster Unionist Party (6), Vanguard Unionist Progressive Party (3)
1979	Democratic Unionist Party (3), Independent Republican (1), Independent Unionist (1), Plaid Cymru (2), Scottish Nationalist Party (2), Ulster Unionist Party (1)
1983	Democratic Unionist Party (3), Plaid Cymru (2), Scottish Nationalist Party (2), Sinn Fein (1), Social Democratic and Labour Party (1), Ulster Popular Unionist Party (1), Ulster Unionist Party (11)
1987	Democratic Unionist Party (3), Plaid Cymru (3), Scottish Nationalist Party (3), Sinn Fein (1), Social Democratic and Labour Party (3), Ulster Popular Unionist Party (1), Ulster Unionist Party (9)
1992	Democratic Unionist Party (3), Plaid Cymru (4), Scottish N Unionist Party (1), Ulster Unionist Party (9)
1997	Democratic Unionist Party (2), Independent (1), Plaid Cymru (4), Scottish Nationalist Party (6), Sinn Fein (2), Social Democratic and Labour Party (3), UK Unionist Party (1), Ulster Unionist Party (10)
2001	Democratic Unionist Party (5), Independent (1), Plaid Cymru (4), Scottish Nationalist Party (5), Sinn Fein (4), Social Democratic and Labour Party (3), Ulster Unionist Party (6)
2005	Democratic Unionist Party (9), Independent (2), Plaid Cymru (3), Scottish Nationalist Party (6), Sinn Fein (5), Social Democratic and Labour Party (3), Ulster Unionist Party (1)

Between 1945 and 1970, Ulster Unionists were included with the Conservative Party

Since 1970, Britain has actually experienced a period of multi-party politics. Although the number of seats won in the House of Commons highlights two parties dominating, when examining the votes cast (see Table 10.4), a different version of events unfolds. Between 1950 and 1970, two parties dominate, winning at least 89% of all votes cast. But from 1974 onwards, the number of votes cast for the smaller parties has increased. With the exception of the 1979 General Election, every election since February 1974 has seen at least one fifth of all votes cast being for parties other than Labour and the Conservatives – and in 1983, 30% of all votes cast were for the Alliance or minor parties. The reason for the quirk of 1979 was the fall in support for the Scottish Nationalists and Plaid Cymru after the failed devolution referendums.

Table 10.4 Percentage of votes won in Post-World War Two General Elections

Year	Conservative	Labour	Liberal*	Others**
1945	39.8	47.8	9.0	3.4
1950	43.5	46.1	9.1	0.7
1951	48.0	48.8	2.5	0.7
1955	49.7	46.4	2.7	1.2
1959	49.4	43.8	5.9	0.9
1964	43.4	44.1	11.2	1.3
1966	41.9	47.9	8.5	1.7
1970	46.4	43.0	7.5	3.1
Feb. 1974	37.9	37.1	19.3	5.7
Oct. 1974	35.8	39.2	18.3	6.7
1979	43.9	36.9	13.8	5.4
1983	42.4	27.6	25.4	4.6
1987	42.3	30.8	22.6	4.3
1992	41.9	34.4	17.8	5.9
1997	30.7	43.2	16.8	9.3
2001	31.7	40.7	18.3	9.3
2005	32.3	35.2	22.0	10.5

* In 1983 and 1987, Liberal figures cover the results for the Liberal/SDP Alliance. The figures for 1992 onwards are for the Liberal Democrats.

* "Others" includes Northern Ireland MPs from Feb. 1974 onwards.

What this table shows is that support for the two major parties has fallen in votes cast. It is a quirk of the electoral system that has enabled the two major parties to survive. Labour in 1983 and the Conservatives in 1997 polled their lowest percentage of votes in the post-war period. Yet, as a result of safe seats and other such phenomena of the Simple Plurality electoral system (see Chapter Eleven), they survived. In both cases, the parties were well ahead of the third placed parties in seats gained, but not in votes received.

At the Parliamentary level, Britain may be portrayed as a two-party system, but it could be argued that Britain is actually a one-party dominant system. After each post-war election (with the exception of February 1974), a single party has dominated Parliament. Some majorities have been huge (Labour in 1945, 1997 and 2001; Conservative in 1959, 1983 and 1987) others have been less so. Yet in every case a single party has formed the Government and has been able to push its' programme through the House. With the larger majorities it has been far easier. During the Thatcher years, and currently with the Blair Government, a single party has dominated electorally and thus in Parliament as well. Radical agendas have been pushed through – privatisation by the Thatcher Government; constitutional reform by the Blair Government – with little or no opposition in the Commons. Any opposition has appeared muted or weak. Thus it is not two-party politics but one-party government.

Conversely, at sub-national levels of government, what is being experienced is often not single party or two party politics but multi-party politics. In the Scottish Parliament and the Northern Ireland Assembly there is coalition government. In the Welsh Assembly, there was a coalition government after the 1999 elections and a tie in 2003 (although with the Speaker coming from an opposition party, it left Labour with a single seat majority). In all three devolved bodies, there is multi-party politics. Both Scotland and Wales have experienced the prospect of almost any party being involved in coalition negotiations, while in Northern Ireland things are even more complicated.

Local government throughout the United Kingdom is even more complicated. Some councils may be dominated by a single party, there may be two-party politics in others, and multi-party politics in other councils. However, nothing is set in stone. Leicester City Council, for example, was Labour controlled from 1979 to 2003. Since the 2003 elections, there has been a Liberal Democrat-Conservative coalition council.

A final point to note about party systems is that there are occasions when a specific issue does not fit party lines. In Britain the most prominent example is the European Union. Traditionally, the major parties adopt opposites – privatisation (Conservative) and nationalisation (Labour); centralisation (Conservative) and devolution (Labour). Most MPs within each party follow their party line happily. This is not the case with Europe. Membership of the

EU cuts across party lines. There may be specified party positions on the EU as presented by each party leadership, but not all members follow them. Within the Conservative Party, there are a minority of MPs who are enthused about Europe (e.g. Ken Clarke) and a number who advocate withdrawal from the EU (e.g. Teddy Taylor). Between these extremes lie a number of perspectives, highlighting differing levels of participation in the EU, some protecting British interests, others advocating greater participation. The Labour Party is no different. There are pro-EU MPs and anti-EU MPs, as well as a range of positions between.

In 1975, when there was a referendum on continued EEC membership, party positions were suspended for the campaign. Those in favour of membership campaigned across party lines, while those opposed to membership did the same. Such cross-party machinations re-occurred during the debates on the Maastricht Treaty in the early 1990s, and appear to be resurfacing in preparation for debates over the Euro and the new EU constitution. The difference to 1975 is that the current cross-party dealings, as with those during the Maastricht legislation, do not have the support of any of the party leaderships. The EU is a complicated issue that clearly does not fit party lines. This makes it even more difficult to classify Britain as a two-party system, especially when it is possible to have Tony Benn and Norman Tebbitt on the same platform, or Ken Clarke and Tony Blair on another.

Conclusion

The British party system is very complicated. In the post-war period there have been two major parties fighting for control of the House of Commons. Yet over the last thirty years, and indeed prior to the Second World War, more than two parties were involved in fighting elections. From the elections of 1974 onwards, multi-party politics appears to be the norm. In Scotland and Wales there is four party politics (although in the case of Scotland, the Greens and the Scottish Socialist Alliance would object to their exclusion), and in Northern Ireland there are even more parties. In England there are three major parties and a plethora of smaller parties and independent candidates. It is at the level of sub-national politics that the smaller parties appear to have a greater influence.

Yet, at the Parliamentary level, we normally see single party government. In the post-war years, power sharing has been the exception rather than the rule. It is single party government, but elections are portrayed as a fight between two rivals – the Conservatives and Labour. These two parties have dominated the post-war electoral scene, hence the perspective of two-party politics in Britain. However, this is to down play the multi-party politics that operates at every election – even in 1951 when the two major parties won almost 97% of the votes cast. The smaller parties may be perceived as no more than a receptacle for protest votes when there is dissatisfaction with the two major parties. Yet it is possible for their policies to be hijacked by the larger parties, as was the case with the Green Party and the issue of the environment in the late 1980s and early 1990s. Added to this, any defeat of a Conservative or Labour incumbent by a minor party or independent candidate is a reminder that they cannot take their supporters votes for granted. In Britain, we may have single party government today, but it is definitely within a context of multi-party politics.

Summary of key points

DEFINITION OF A POLITICAL PARTY

❑ A group of like-minded thinkers who fight elections in an attempt to gain Office

❑ Political parties tend to be underpinned by an ideology – a system of values and beliefs that can be used to explain events or form the basis for policies

THE CASE FOR BRITAIN STILL HAVING A TWO PARTY SYSTEM

❑ Parliament is structured around a two-party system – Government and Opposition

❑ In the post-war era, two parties have alternated in Government

❑ Two parties have dominated election results and representation in Parliament

THE CASE AGAINST BRITAIN STILL HAVING A TWO PARTY SYSTEM

❑ Since the 1970s there has been a marked decrease in support for the two major parties, especially in votes cast

❑ It is the vagaries of the electoral system that enable the two major parties to dominate Westminster

❑ Multi-party politics in sub-national government (regional and local)

❑ Not all issues fit the two-party model e.g. Europe

Further Reading

Barneris, P., McHugh, J., and Tyldesley, M.; *Encyclopedia of British and Irish Political Organisations* (Pinter 2000)

Ingle, S.; *The British Party System* (Pinter 2000) 3rd edition

McNaughton, N.; "The Changing Nature of UK Political Parties" *Talking Politics* vol. 15, 2003

Webb, P.; *The Modern British Party System* (Sage 2000)

Wilde, E.; "The Recent History of the Conservative Party" *Talking Politics* vol. 15, 2002

Internet sites

www.conservatives-party.org.uk

Homepage of the Conservative Party

www.labour.org.uk

Homepage of the Labour Party

www.libdems.org.uk

Homepage of the Liberal Democratic Party

www.plaidcymru.org

Homepage of Plaid Cymru

www.psr.keele.ac.uk/area/uk/e01/parties2001.htm

This web page contains a list of all parties who had candidates standing in the 2001 General Election as well as independent candidates, with links to some of the parties and candidates

www.snp.org.uk

Homepage of the Scottish Nationalist Party

CHAPTER ELEVEN

Elections

INTRODUCTION

The electoral system is the set of rules by which the people select their representatives. There are many features to an electoral system, the most important of which are the district magnitude (number of representatives per constituency), the type of ballot (how the voters cast their votes e.g. a single categoric choice, multiple choices, ranking of preferences, and so on), and the electoral formula (how the votes are translated into representation). In effect, different electoral systems can be derived from various combinations of these three electoral rules alone – and there are many other rules as well (see Lijphart 1985). Thus the British system for Parliamentary elections is Simple Plurality (sometimes referred to as First-Past-the-Post). There are single member constituencies, with voters casting a single categoric choice, and the candidate with the most votes is declared the winner.

Election

A system whereby people cast their votes for candidates or parties to select their representatives. There are a vast number of ways for votes to be cast (type of ballot), and for the votes to be translated into representation (electoral formula).

However, this is not the only electoral system in use in Britain. Different systems are used in other tiers of government – party lists for mainland Britain's elections to the European Parliament; Mixed Member-Proportional (MMP) for the Scottish Parliament, the Welsh Assembly and the Greater London Authority; the Single Transferable Vote (STV) for all elections in the Northern Ireland; the Supplementary Vote for the mayor of London; and the Block Vote for some councils in England. This chapter is not going to examine all of these electoral systems in great detail. This has been done elsewhere (see Cocker and Jones (2002), Farrell (2001), Lakeman (1982) and Reeve and Ware (1992)). However, it is important to know of their existence. Simple Plurality is not the only electoral system in use in the United Kingdom, although the way some pundits talk, you might think otherwise.

Britain's Parliamentary electoral system of Simple Plurality is normally portrayed as an important feature of democracy. This idea of democracy has voters going to their polling booths and electing a local representative. However, the continued use of this electoral system is coming under great pressure. The Blair Government promised a commission into electoral reform after the 1997 General Election. This was headed by Lord Jenkins. The commission was given a clear remit to recommend an alternative system to Simple Plurality, and these would be run off against each other in a referendum. The requirements are laid out in Table 11.1. It is important to note that none of these were considered to be absolute.

Table 11.1 The requirements to be taken into account by the Jenkins Commission

Broad proportionality

The need for a stable government

An extension of voter choice

The maintenance of a link between MPs and a geographical constituency

The Jenkins Commission eventually proposed an electoral system called AV Plus, sometimes called AV Top Up. AV stands for the Alternative Vote – an electoral system which is used in Australia. However, AV Plus is a hybrid electoral system, not too dissimilar to MMP. There are two parts to the ballot. In the first, there are single member constituencies where voters rank the candidates in order of preference. To gain election, the leading candidate requires an absolute majority of the votes cast (i.e. over 50%). Should no candidate achieve this target, then the last placed candidate is eliminated and his/her votes are redistributed according to the next listed preference. This process continues until the leading candidate gains an absolute majority of votes cast in the constituency.

The second part of the election is the 'top up', which is used to ensure some degree of proportionality. Jenkins envisaged around 15-20% of MPs to be elected as the top up. The UK would be divided into regions, each electing one or two extra MPs. The formula for allocating the top up was:

$$\frac{\text{Votes cast for a party in a region}}{\text{Seats won by that party in that region} + 1}$$

The party with the highest number after this mathematical equation gains the first top up seat. If need be, the mathematics is then recalculated for that party to see who gains the second top up seat.

After a fanfare of publicity at the time of publication, this report appears to have disappeared from the political agenda. Even the death of Lord Jenkins in early 2003 did not re-ignite the debate around this proposed electoral system. Apart from the Liberal Democrats, nobody appears interested in electoral reform for Parliamentary elections. Even though some parties have benefited from such reforms in other elections, support for any sort of electoral reform appears muted.

Do We Need Electoral Reform in Britain?
The case against electoral reform

The basic premise for retaining Simple Plurality is "if it ain't broke, don't fix it". The system works. It is a simple, easy to understand method of voting. The voter goes to the polling booth and places a mark next to the candidate of their choice. The candidate who wins the most votes is elected as representative of that constituency. Arguably, alternative means of casting ballots could be used – and this is currently under investigation by the government. Rather than going to the polling booth, why not cast your ballot by post, e-mail or text message. Each of these options, and others, is under investigation in an attempt to increase voter turnout. However, the electoral system itself remains unchanged. Of all the electoral systems in use around the world, Simple Plurality is probably the most straightforward of them all.

Simple Plurality has also provided stability to British Government, not only throughout the post-war period but since the modern system of party politics came into being. The major parties are all broad coalitions – umbrella organizations that cover a wide range of ideas. There is less danger of extreme parties gaining election under Simple Plurality – particularly at the Parliamentary level. The Communist Party gained two MPs in 1945 but has never really been a serious electoral threat. To the other extreme, fascist parties such as the BNP have never gained election to the British Parliament. In the 2005 General Election, the BNP polled their highest percentage of votes in a single constituency (16.9% in the constituency of Barking). However, they were still a distant third place.

The danger of extremism can be compared to countries which use systems of proportional representation, where extremist parties have often not only gained election but have also been in positions to hold the country to ransom through coalition building. Examples include the Italian party Abolizione

Scorporo, one of whose deputies is Alessandra Mussolini; the Vlaams Blok in Belgium; Lijst Pim Fortuyn in the Netherlands; the Austrian Freedom Party formerly led by Jurg Haider; the Free Democrats in Germany; and some of the religious parties in Israel.

Not only does this stable electoral system used in Britain usually prevent extremist parties from gaining representation, but it also tends to result in strong, single party governments. As noted in the previous chapter, in the post-war period there has only been one occasion (February 1974) where a single party has not won a general election outright – and even on that occasion there was a minority government rather than a coalition. With a single party in power it is able to implement its manifesto programme. This is normally the basis upon which the party fought the election. Coalitions, on the other hand, often see extended periods of negotiations with the potential coalition partners haggling over which manifesto pledges can be watered down or dropped altogether. An example of such extended coalition negotiations was in New Zealand after the 1996 General Election. This was the first election held under the MMP electoral system. The negotiations lasted around nine weeks between the New Zealand First Party (which came third) and both the National and Labour parties. The leader of New Zealand First, Winston Peters, played the two other parties off against each other in an attempt to get the best possible deal for his party. Such problems are considered to be symptomatic of any form of proportional representation but are very rare indeed under Simple Plurality.

What also results under the Simple Plurality system is a clear alternative to the government. The leading opposition party is able to portray itself as an alternative government – a government-in-waiting. This is an important aspect of the adversarial system that is generated under Simple Plurality. If the government of the day is not to your liking or is performing poorly, it is possible to vote them out of office. Under proportional electoral systems, with coalition governments, it is not so easily done. In fact, it is possible for parties to stay in office by forming new coalitions with other parties e.g. Christian Democrats in Italy. Thus it is far more difficult to remove a party from office under proportional electoral systems than it is under Simple Plurality.

A final aspect of the advantages of Simple Plurality is the MP-constituency link. Under Simple Plurality, each constituency elects a single representative. Thus Keith Vaz is the MP for Leicester East. It is his job to represent all of the constituents in Leicester East, regardless of their political persuasion. This also means that if he does a poor job for his constituency, he could be removed at a subsequent election. Very few other electoral systems have single member constituencies. Some have multi-member constituencies (STV and the Block Vote, for example), while others may have national or regional lists. In each of these cases, voters may have the opportunity to play candidates from the same party against each other. After an election, constituents may play their representatives off against each other, regardless of their political party. There may be no consistency in this representation. A single representative may also be held to account far more easily. Under a party list, the party is able to position the candidates on the lists and voters may not have the chance to change this. Such a situation occurred in Britain for the elections to the European Parliament, where a closed regional party list system was used. The political parties placed the candidates in order of election and the voters had no opportunity to rearrange them. Arguably this undermined any link between candidates and constituency.

In sum, the current system of Simple Plurality appears to work well for British Parliamentary elections. Methods of voting could be changed or modernized by the electoral system itself functions effectively. Voters cast their ballots for the individual who they would most like to represent them. Their votes only apply in the constituency in which they are cast. The results tend to enable a strong government to implement its' election manifesto. Coalition governments are a most unlikely result, and are viewed with disdain. The idea of sharing power and diluting manifesto programmes, without consulting the electorate is not a feature of the modern British Parliament. Deals behind closed doors, in smoke-filled back rooms are not considered to be an acceptable feature of government. A government needs to be accountable to the people. The manifesto programme is the list of promises by which a government is elected, and can be the yardstick to judge success. Failure to achieve goals can result in the government losing the subsequent election.

The case for electoral reform

While Britain's Parliamentary electoral system appears to give a veneer of effectiveness, the reality is significantly different. Even some of the arguments used to defend the system are flawed. The idea that the current electoral system provides stability needs to be questioned. In the post–war period there have been three occasions where a second general election was held within eighteen months of an earlier one – 1950 and 1951; 1964 and 1966; and February and October 1974. Elections can be hugely disruptive to Parliamentary life, as well as life in general. Successive elections over such short periods of time mean that parties are unable to implement even parts of their manifesto programme.

Even when there is a large Parliamentary majority, it does not guarantee stability. The Thatcher and Blair Governments have had huge majorities in the number of seats won at Westminster, but only on a plurality of the vote. The last occasion where a government won an absolute majority of votes was in 1935. Thus a majority of voters are not seeing the programme that they voted for being implemented. When these programmes are more radical – such as Thatcher's policies on privatization and reducing the role of the State, or Blair's on constitutional reform – a large number of people may actually be dissatisfied. The Thatcher Government used Scotland as a guinea pig for the introduction of the Community Charge (Poll Tax) in the late 1980s. At that time the Conservatives held very few seats in Scotland. Thus the electoral damage of this policy, in Scotland at least, was expected to be minimal to the Conservatives, even though the outcry was considerable. Added to this, when there is a change in government, the policies of the previous incumbent can be reversed. This was most noticeable with the changes in government in the 1960s and 1970s – in particular on disputed policy areas such as between private ownership and nationalization.

In blunt terms, Simple Plurality distorts electoral results. While each constituency has a single representative, and the party with the most representatives wins the election, this actually leads to artificially large majorities which often bear little resemblance to the votes cast across the country (see Table 11.2). The percentage of votes gained across the country tends to bear little resemblance to the percentage of seats held in Parliament by the two major parties. In every election since 1964, the Labour Party has had a much higher percentage of seats held in comparison to votes won. So even when the Labour Party vote collapsed in 1983, they were still able to hold on to a much higher percentage of seats. The same applies to the Conservatives between 1950 and 1992 (except 1966) where the percentage of seats held has been higher than the percentage of votes gained. In the last general election we saw the biggest ever discrepancy with Labour winning 62.7% of the seats on a national vote of 40.7%, and that is before touching upon the turnout of 59.4%. If turnout were to be included then the Blair Government won almost two thirds of the seats on around a quarter of the potential vote.

What Simple Plurality does encourage is an adversarial two-party system. The way in which elections are presented to the public is in such a manner. Peter Snow prances around on our television screens with his swingometer – if the Conservative gain such a percentage of votes from Labour then the pendulum will move in such a manner and the new Parliament will look like so. This focuses upon the supposed straight fight between the Conservatives and Labour. All other parties are marginalized – or, more accurately, ignored. This discrimination against smaller parties will be examined below. The adversarial approach to British politics, as noted earlier, undermines the stability of the political system. It is a confrontational approach. The two parties are expected to oppose each other. This gives the voter the straight choice. However, in the 1997 election, Labour Party fears were such that they proposed to stick to the Conservative spending plans for the first two years of their government.

Table 11.2 Percentage of votes won and seats held in the post-war period

Year	Conservative		Labour	
	% votes	% seats	% votes	% seats
1945	39.8	33.3	47.8	61.4
1950	43.5	47.7	46.1	50.4
1951	48.0	51.4	48.8	47.2
1955	49.7	54.6	46.4	44.0
1959	49.4	57.9	43.8	41.0
1964	43.4	48.3	44.1	50.3
1966	41.9	40.1	47.9	57.6
1970	46.4	52.4	43.0	45.6
1974 (Feb.)	37.9	46.8	37.1	47.4
1974 (Oct.)	35.8	43.6	39.2	50.2
1979	43.9	53.4	36.9	42.4
1983	42.4	61.1	27.6	32.2
1987	42.3	57.7	30.8	35.2
1992	41.9	51.6	34.4	41.6
1997	30.7	25.0	43.2	63.6
2001	31.7	25.2	40.7	62.7
2005	32.3	30.5	35.2	55.2

Not only is a two-party system encouraged, but at the same time the other parties are discriminated against. The British public is gradually becoming aware of this concern. In the 1983 General Election the SDP–Liberal Alliance won 25.4% of the votes cast but only 23 seats. The Labour Party won 27.6% of the votes and 209 seats. Although this is the most extreme example, similar scenarios can be presented in every general election since February 1974.

Discrimination also occurs, as a result of the use of Simple Plurality, on grounds of ethnicity and gender. In 1997, more women were elected to Westminster than ever before – 120 female MPs – but this dropped to 118 in 2001 before rising to 128 in 2005. In the 2001 General Election, 12 ethnic minority MPs gained election. This under representation of women and ethnic minority MPs cannot be directly attributed to the electoral system. However as a result of the focus on a two-party system, parties tend to select "safe" candidates and these are invariably white males (see Chapter Nineteen on Gender).

In an attempt to address these discrepancies against the smaller parties and against women and ethnic minorities, proportional electoral systems have been used for elections to other bodies. These include the European Parliament as well as the elections to the devolved bodies in Scotland, Wales and Northern Ireland, and to the Greater London Authority. In every case, many smaller parties have gained some degree of representation in the elected bodies (see Table 11.3). Thus not only do we see the Liberal Democrats in coalition government in Scotland, but also the Greens gaining representation in Scotland and London. Plaid Cymru and the Scottish Nationalist Party are the official opposition parties in their devolved bodies. Independent candidates gained election in Scotland and Wales, while the Scottish Socialist Alliance increased its number of MSPs (Members of the Scottish Parliament) in 2003. In the Northern Ireland Assembly election of 1998, nine parties gained representation. Finally, the UK Independence Party gained representation in the European Parliament, as did the Greens the SNP, Plaid Cymru and the Liberal Democrats.

Table 11.3 Minor Party Representation in Britain outside of Parliament and local government (as of July 2004)

Party	Bodies to which they have been elected (Number of elected representatives)
Green Party	European Parliament (2), Greater London Authority (2), Scottish Parliament (6)
Liberal Democrats	European Parliament (12), Greater London Authority (5), Scottish Parliament (17), Welsh Assembly (6)
Plaid Cymru	Welsh Assembly (12), European Parliament (1)
Scottish Nationalist Party	Scottish Parliament (27), European Parliament (2)
Scottish Socialist Alliance	Scottish Parliament (5)
UK Independence Party	European Parliament (12), Greater London Authority (2)
Independent candidates	Scottish Parliament (4), Welsh Assembly (1)

With regard to the representation of women, the Welsh Assembly became the first such body to have 50% women elected in 2003. This surpasses the previous 'high' of 42% in the Swedish Parliament. The Scottish Parliament was not so successful, although it did increase the level of female representation to 50 MSPs (38.8%). In London, eleven of the 25 members of the London Assembly are women.

The elections to the European Parliament were as problematic as Simple Plurality. Closed party lists were used. This meant that the political parties were able to rank their candidates in order, not the voters. Consequently, "safe" candidates predominated. In the 1999 European Parliamentary elections, 24% of British MEPs were female. While this is higher than Westminster (18%) it highlights the problem of the control of parties rather than the electoral choices of voters.

As for ethnic minority representation, there are 4 MEPs and one member of the London Assembly who represent ethnic minorities. This is a somewhat higher percentage than is represented in Parliament but is still below the number of ethnic minorities in the UK today. There is no ethnic minority representation in either the Scottish Parliament or the Welsh Assembly.

A final point on why electoral reform is essential for elections to Westminster can be summarized under the label of 'fairness'. While this may seem a rather insignificant aspect when examining the merits of an electoral system, it is still worth noting. When an electoral system throws up such absurd results as have occurred in the last few elections, then it is imperative that the whole democratic structure upon which it is built ought to be re-examined in the light of the essential element of democracy. Why should a party be able to hold near absolute power when it fails to win an absolute majority of the votes cast? On three occasions, a party has won an election while gaining less than 40% of the vote (February and October 1974 and 2005) – hence Lord Hailsham's argument of "Elective Dictatorship". It is even possible to win a general election without necessarily winning the most votes – as happened in 1951 and February 1974.

Conclusion

Electoral reform is a problematic issue in British politics. While such reform is readily implemented at sub-national government, and for elections to the European Parliament, whenever it is suggested for Parliament, there is a huge outcry. Electoral reform is portrayed as a monumental shift away from the traditional patterns of British politics. It is also assumed that electoral reform means adopting some form of proportional representation – which is not necessarily the case. This can be seen in the multi-dimensional approach to electoral reform presented in Table 11.4. Basically, electoral reform means changing the electoral system – it does not have to be to some form of proportional representation, there are many other alternatives.

Table 11.4 A Multi-Dimensional Approach to the Classification of Electoral Systems

Classification	District Magnitude	Type of Ballot	Formula
Plurality	Single member Multi-member	Single vote Multiple votes (votes = seats)	Simple Plurality Block Vote
Majoritarian	Single member	Single vote Rank preferences Multiple vote (votes = candidates) Multiple vote (votes < candidates)	Second Ballot Condorcet Borda Alternative Vote Supplementary Vote Approval Voting Exhaustive Voting
Semi-proportional	Multi-member	Single vote Rank preferences Multiple vote (votes < seats)	Single Non-Transferable Vote Cumulative Vote Limited Vote
Proportional	Multi-member	Rank preferences Party list (any of:) open closed flexible panachage	Single Transferable Vote d'Hondt Imperiali St. Lague Niemeyer Hagenbach-Bischoff
Hybrid	Single member (with top up) Single and multi-member	Single vote Two votes: one for a candidate one for a list	Additional Member System Mixed Member- Proportional AV Top Up

Added to this, there is a fixation upon the electoral formula – the method of translating votes into seats – and the label (proportional, majoritarian, etc.) It might actually be more constructive to focus upon the number of representatives in a constituency, or how voters cast their ballots. These two areas are probably less divisive than the formula or the categorisation to be used. It may also be possible to find or create an electoral system that actually appeals to both those in favour and those opposed to electoral reform (although noting the intransigence of the latter, this is most unlikely).

The problem is that all electoral systems have their flaws. If there is to be electoral reform, then it will take time to bed down. In New Zealand, MMP replaced Simple Plurality in 1996. They have just had their third election under MMP. It has taken this long for the voting population to adjust their mindset as to how the electoral system functions, and the role of the voter within this. Only now is it feasible to audit the success of MMP in New Zealand in a credible manner. If there is ever to be electoral reform in Britain, the same needs to apply. Change for one or two elections before reverting back to Simple Plurality will achieve little. As with all change, it takes time for people to adjust. Electoral reform, should it occur, will have profound effects upon not just Parliament, but all of Britain.

Summary of key points

DEFINITION OF ELECTION

❏   A system whereby people select their representatives

❏   There are many different electoral systems, each with their own specific rules on: how votes are cast (type of ballot); how many representatives are elected from a constituency (district magnitude); how votes are translated into representation (electoral formula)

❏   Currently in Britain six different electoral systems are used at different tiers of government: Simple Plurality, d'Hondt party list, STV, MMP, Supplementary Vote, and the Block Vote

THE CASE AGAINST ELECTORAL REFORM

❏   Simple Plurality provides a stable system for Westminster Governments

❏   It is a straight forward, easy to understand electoral system

❏   Simple Plurality makes it very difficult for extremist parties to gain election

❏   It encourages a strong MP-constituency link

THE CASE FOR ELECTORAL REFORM

❏   Stability arguments are flawed – there is a huge potential for shake up at each election

❏   In the overall result, there is limited relationship between votes won and seats gained at Westminster

❑   Simple Plurality encourages adversarial politics
❑   Many non-Westminster elections no longer use Simple Plurality, with
    little adverse effects

Further Reading

Cocker, P. and Jones, A.; *Contemporary British Politics and Government* (Liverpool
Academic Press 2002) esp. chapter 6.

Farrell, D.; *Electoral Systems: A Comparative Introduction* (Palgrave 2001)

Lakeman, E.; *Power to Elect: The Case for Proportional Representation* (Heinemann
1982)

Lijphart, A.; "The Field of Electoral Systems Research: A Critical Survey"
Electoral Studies vol. 4, 1985

Reeve, A. and Ware, A.; *Electoral Systems: A Comparative and Theoretical
Introduction* (Routledge 1992)

Internet sites

dodgson.ucsd.edu/lij/

Homepage of the Lijphart Elections Archive at the University of California,
San Diego

www.electionresources.org

This web page contains a database of countries and their election results from
around the world

www.electoralcommission.org.uk/

Home page of the British Electoral Commission

www.psr.keele.ac.uk/election.htm

This site contains elections and electoral systems from around the world. The
website is based at Keele University

CHAPTER TWELVE
Voting Behaviour

INTRODUCTION

The topic of voting behaviour is often perceived as being very complicated. Part of the problem stems from the fact that the information being dealt with is of a second-hand nature. Experts are dependent upon voters telling the truth about how their ballots were cast. An often cited apocryphal tale is of the 1992 General Election where the number of people who claimed to have voted Labour far outstretched the number that actually did. Had all those who claimed to have voted Labour actually done so then Labour would have probably won the election.

> ### *Voting behaviour*
>
> At its most basic level, this is how people vote. However, voting behaviour can be analysed by a number of competing factors including: class, ethnicity, gender, age, employment status and home ownership. Issues may also influence how people vote e.g. the war in Iraq, the war on terror, immigration, the environment, etc.

Added to this problem of second-hand information is the range of factors that may impact upon how people vote. Table 12.1 presents a list of factors that may influence how people cast their ballots. These potential factors are divided into four sections. The first of these is 'Personal Factors'. This covers the personal beliefs and attitudes that may influence how people vote. Secondly there are the 'Social Factors'. These focus upon the socialisation of voters – the influence of family and friends, as well as other factors such as age, ethnicity and gender. Next there are the 'Political Factors'. This focuses upon the election; who is involved in fighting it (parties and candidates), as well as the issues involved in the election. Finally, there are the 'Other Factors'. These are the miscellaneous factors that may have an impact upon how people vote. Included here are such things as the role of the media and the weather.

Table 12.1 Factors that may influence voting behaviour

PERSONAL FACTORS	Status crystallisation	Class consciousness, or awareness of social status
	Attitudes	Personal beliefs or feelings
	Marginality	Extent of integration into society
	Isolation	Absence of social pressures
	Sense of efficacy	Beliefs about personal abilities to change things
	Alienation	Lack of involvement with social structures
	Anomie	Lack of involvement with social norms
	Psychic gratification	Positive or negative feelings about performing social duties
	Cross-pressures	Impact of conflicting messages or social beliefs
	Ideology	Personal and social belief system
	Personal influence	Ability to influence others
	Membership of groups	Range of social contacts
	Personalities of leaders	Evaluation of political leaders
	Performance evaluation	Views of performance of parties, leaders, etc.
SOCIAL FACTORS	Family and socialisation	Effect of living environment and upbringing
	Religion	Impact of religious beliefs
	Race	Impact of ethnic status
	Age	Effect of age on perceptions
	Gender	Effect of gender and gender differences
	Social mobility	Changes in voter status
	Socio-economic status	Location in class structure of society
	Consumption location	Personal interpretation of social status and group interests
POLITICAL FACTORS	Type of election	Impact of type of election (e.g. local, national, etc.) and willingness to vote
	Safety of seat	How marginal is the seat (likelihood of incumbent losing)
	Electoral rules	Eligibility to vote

	Partisanship	Strength of loyalty to a particular party or candidate
	National issues	Effect of national issues on local choices
	Number of parties	Range of options in casting ballot
	External political stimuli	Effect of 'social' and 'other' factors
	Tactical voting	Effect of electoral rules on how a ballot may be cast
OTHER FACTORS	Mass media	Effect of reporting of issues, campaign or personalities that induces people to cast their ballot in a particular manner
	Propaganda	Campaign tactics to induce people to support or oppose parties or candidates
	Opinion polls	Effect of information in confirming or changing electors voting intentions
	Weather	Impact of climate on ability or willingness to vote
	Urban/rural divide	Effect of type of environment
	'Big City' factor	Extra effect arising from living in London or other large cities
	Position on ballot paper	Effect and consequences of the format and location of candidates on the ballot paper

As can be seen in Table 12.1, there is an extensive list of factors. However, it is important to note that not all of them may have an impact in every election. Some of these factors may drift in and out of explanations. They may even be interlinked. Thus the socialisation of people living in rural North Scotland will be very different to that of people living in Moss Side in Manchester. The 'personal' and 'social' factors will be very different, as well as the role of some of the 'other' factors.

Yet, despite this extensive list of potential factors that may influence voting behaviour, one factor has been highlighted as an explanatory of British voting patterns – class. Peter Pulzer stated in 1967 that "Class is the basis of British party politics; all else is embellishment and detail". Between 1950 and 1970, class did indeed appear to be the best explanation as to how people voted. This was the period of class alignment, where the majority of working class people (around 65%) voted Labour and the majority of the middle class (around 80%) voted Conservative. There was much evidence to support Pulzers' claim.

However, since 1970 class appears to have become less important in explaining voting behaviour. The period from 1970 to the late 1980s has been described as class dealignment. The strong link between class and voting behaviour had decreased. Today, as ever, opinion is divided as to the extent of the importance of class in explaining voting behaviour.

Does class still explain voting behaviour?

The case for class as an explanation of voting behaviour

When presenting the case for class as an explanation of voting behaviour, an important proviso must be noted. Quite simply, it is no longer the case that class is the sole explanation as to how people vote. Rather it is still a major factor in explaining how people vote.

The periods of class alignment and de-alignment hinged upon a very narrow definition of class. It was based upon the profession of the head of the household i.e. the husband or father. Thus all women and any children were classified according to the profession of the 'alpha male'. Using the British Market Research Society (BMRS) classifications (see Table 12.2), if a labourer (unskilled manual labour, social class D) was married to a school teacher (non-manual employee, social class B), the household would be classified as a working class household.

Table 12.2 British Marketing Research Society division of class

Class	Categorisation	Explanation
Middle	A	Higher Professional, Managerial and Administrative
	B	Middle Professional, Managerial and Administrative
	CI	Other Non-Manual
Working	C2	Skilled Manual Workers
	D	Semi-Skilled and Unskilled Workers
	E	State Dependents

As noted in Chapter Two (Political Culture), Britain is still a class-based society. Although the importance of class may have diminished, it is still an important feature of Britain and British politics. What has changed, and is constantly changing, is the way in which class is defined. The BMRS approach is often viewed as being a little dated, not only in focusing upon the head of the household but also in being unable to keep up with technological developments that may have out-dated some of the class labels. Tables 12.3 and 12.4 present alternative methods of classifying people according to their class.

Table 12.3 Heath, Jowell and Curtice definition of class

Salariat Managers, supervisors, professionals
Routine Non-manual Clerks, sales workers, secretaries
Petit Bourgeoisie Farmers, small proprietors, self-employed manual workers
Foreman, Technicians Blue collar supervisory class
Working Class Manual workers in industry and agriculture (Regardless of skill levels, what distinguishes this 'class' status is that they are subject to detailed supervision)

(Developed from Heath, Jowell and Curtice; *How Britain Votes* (1985))

The Heath, Jowell and Curtice approach was introduced in an attempt to re-evaluate class dealignment. They argued that the fundamental changes in the relative size of the social classes had been ignored. In their opinion, Britain had become a more white-collar (middle class) society. Consequently there had been a decline in support for the Labour Party. To address this situation, Heath, Jowell and Curtice offered a structure of class that was based more upon specific occupations.

Although this approach was not favoured by many academics, it did highlight the need for a possible re-evaluation into the way class was defined. The underlying premise was that class still mattered as an explanation of voting behaviour.

In 1997 the Economic and Social Research Council (ESRC) proposed an alternative form of the classification of class. The first thing to note about this approach was that it was very much job-specific – far more so than the Heath, Jowell and Curtice approach. It highlighted the changes in employment patterns that have occurred in Britain over the last couple of decades and was not tied down to the head of the household approach.

Table 12.4 Economic and Social Research Council classification of class

1. Doctors, lawyers, scientists, and employers, administrators and managers in 'large' organisations, i.e. those with 25 or more staff
2. Nurses, legal executives, laboratory technicians, other 'associate professionals', employers, administrators and managers in smaller organisations, supervisors of intermediate staff
3. Secretaries, sales reps, nursery nurses, computer operators and other intermediate occupations in administrative, clerical, sales and service work
4. Driving instructors, builders, carpenters and other self-employed non-professionals
5. Telephone fitters, plumbers and other supervisors and crafts and related works
6. Lorry drivers, assembly line workers, traffic wardens and workers in routine occupations in manufacturing and services
7. "All types of labourers, waiters and waitresses and cleaners" and other workers in elementary occupations in manufacturing and services
8. The underclass of those who have never worked and the long-term unemployed and sick

(Developed from *The Guardian,* 15 December 1997)

Yet again, this re evaluation of class categories suggests that class does matter. Elections throughout the 1980s and 1990s focussed upon class. The Thatcher and Major governments attempted to target a particular class (the C2 class) in their election campaigns. This particular class is the largest using the BMRS approach. Traditionally, the C2s were perceived as Labour supporters – the skilled working class. In the 1980s, successive Thatcher Governments attempted to woo this particular class by enhancing their aspirations and then trying to meet them. Thus there was the sale of council houses and the privatisation of most nationalised industries. Thatcher wanted to create a share-owning, home-owning class that had all the mod cons. This was a very individualistic approach, often symbolised by Del Boy in the television sitcom 'Only Fools and Horses', where "by Christmas we'll be millionaires".

The Labour Party under Blair has also targeted a particular class. Whereas the Conservatives successfully won over a large number of the skilled working class, Labour has focussed upon winning over the middle classes – symbolised by Worcester Man and Worcester Woman. Thus the first Blair Government pledged to stick to the Conservatives spending plans and not to increase direct taxes. The objective was to gain the trust of the middle classes. While the

Labour Party has been very successful in doing this, it appears to be at the expense of their traditional supporters – the working class. It may have been easier for the Conservatives in that they appeared to be giving the working class the opportunity to become middle class. Since the 2001 General Election, moves have been afoot, led by some trades unions, to bring the Labour Party back to the working class. There is a feeling that it has become a pseudo-middle class alternative Conservative Party, which favours big business over the traditional rank and file workers.

A final point to note is that while class may have decreased in importance, no other factor has been able to replace it as an adequate explanation of voting behaviour. While it is possible to examine patterns of urban and rural support, or age, ethnicity or gender in examining voting behaviour, the class link always appears. In some cases, it may be the 'deviant' voters e.g. working class Tories or middle class Socialists, but the fact of the matter is that class still matters.

The case against class as an explanation of voting behaviour

Class has clearly declined in importance when it comes to explaining voting behaviour, to the extent that it is no longer a convincing approach when explaining British voting behaviour. As already noted earlier in this chapter, there have been a number of attempts to redefine the various classes. The BMRS approach, as detailed in Table 12.2 is considered to be out of date. The redefinition presented by Heath, Jowell and Curtice gained little favour. Close examination of Table 12.3 shows that the petit bourgeoisie classification actually includes professions that have been traditionally viewed as middle and working class, with proprietors and self-employed manual workers being compressed under the same label.

The latest approach by the ESRC (Table 12.4) is even more complicated. It merely details different types of employment, and lumps similar professions together. It is rather peculiar to see plumbers separated from carpenters and builders, with the plumbers being the lower class. All that the ESRC approach highlights is the wide range of types of employment that actually exist today. It is rather difficult to label each section as a different class. Plumbers, carpenters and builders are all skilled manual workers. If anything, the approach is too job specific to enable anyone to draw meaningful links with voting behaviour.

Not only is there a difficulty in defining class, but the fact of the matter is that class has declined in importance. The idea during the period of alignment was that the majority of the working class voted Labour and the majority of the middle class voted Conservative. However, this is based on a premise of a two party system. As noted in Chapter Ten (Political Parties), there is a very convincing argument that Britain now has multi-party politics. A two class system with a specific party representing each class has been surpassed. The Liberal Democrats take similar levels of support from all classes (see Table 12.5).

Table 12.5 Vote by Social Class in 2001 (1997) in percentages

Party	AB	CI	C2	DE
Labour	33 (31)	39 (37)	47 (50)	50 (57)
Conservative	40 (41)	35 (37)	29 (27)	27 (21)
Liberal Democrat	21 (22)	20 (18)	18 (16)	18 (13)

Source: Developed from *The Observer,* 10 June 2001

What is peculiar when examining voting in the last two elections is the increase in middle class support for Labour between 1997 and 2001, and the increase in working class support for the Conservatives and the Liberal Democrats over the same time period. The class factor is clearly diminishing.

As class has decreased in importance, other factors have gained credence as explanations of voting behaviour. Table 12.1 contained a huge list of potential factors that may influence how people vote. Not all of them necessarily apply to any election, but some are gaining in importance. What is also important to note is that regional and local issues may actually play an important part in voting behaviour. In Scotland and Wales there is four party politics, with the Scottish Nationalists and Plaid Cymru playing very important roles in their respective countries. In Northern Ireland, electoral politics is mostly fought along sectarian lines rather than by class.

Local issues may also be important. In the constituency of Wyre Forest, the issue was keeping the Kidderminster Hospital Accident and Emergency unit open. This galvanised local opinion, with an Independent candidate (Richard Taylor) winning the seat in 2001 with 58.1% of the vote (on a constituency turnout of 68%). While this may appear unusual, the local factors in this particular case go much deeper. Kidderminster Council was under the control of the Independent Kidderminster Save Our Hospital councillors. Richard Taylor fought the general election campaign under the same banner. This was clearly an important local issue – added to which the Labour candidate was a junior minister in the Department of Health. Particular local issues may affect specific constituencies. These issues tend to be unrelated to class. The closure of an Accident and Emergency unit affects the entire community.

A final point to note is the lack of voting behaviour. The 2001 General Election had the poorest turnout since 1918 at 59.4%. The post–war average turnout prior to 2001 was 76.7%. It was a significant drop on the previous lowest turnout in the post–war era of 72% in 1970. The poor turnout suggests a lack of interest in voting. It is still unclear whether such a low turnout is due to apathy and disinterest in Westminster politics, or a deliberate decision by people to withhold their votes in protest. There was a suggestion that the turnout in Scotland and Wales was lower because there was a closer link to the Scottish Parliament and the Welsh Assembly. However, the turnouts for the 2003 elections to the devolved bodies were also very low (in Wales it was 38.2%). With turnouts decreasing, the politicians need to find ways to stimulate or motivate the voting public into casting their ballots.

What has also been important, particularly in recent general elections has been tactical voting. In 1997 in many constituencies there was a feeling of 'get the Tories out'. People cast their ballots for the candidate most likely to defeat the Conservative incumbent. This was one of the reasons for the huge landslide against the Conservatives. In the 2001 General Election, such tactical voting continued. Some of it was more orchestrated. Labour campaigner, Billy Bragg, encouraged people to vote out Oliver Letwin, the Conservative MP for West Dorset by voting for the Liberal Democrats. In Southwest Norfolk, the Liberal Democrat candidate, Gordon Dean, encouraged his supporters to vote Labour in an attempt to unseat the Conservative incumbent, Gillian Sheppard. Both campaigns were unsuccessful. Letwin won with a reduced majority while Sheppard actually increased hers.

A final factor that needs to be noted is the role of the media. The manner in which the media reports issues, particularly at election time is very important. The role of the media will be examined in greater detail in Chapter Seventeen. However, some points need to be noted in respect to influencing voting behaviour.

The broadcast media is expected to be impartial and balanced in respect of reporting political events. The major parties should receive parity in their electoral coverage, with the smaller parties gaining coverage in line with earlier electoral success. The print media, on the other hand, is biased. Specific newspapers openly support and show bias towards particular political parties and individuals. The Sun conducted a vitriolic campaign against former Labour Party leader Neil Kinnock, and in 1992 claimed to have won the general election for John Major, with the headline "It was the Sun wot won it". In the subsequent three elections, this same newspaper has backed Blair (rather than the Labour Party). Newspaper readership does have some influence over political attitudes and voting behaviour. Already a number of papers are campaigning to protect the pound and to stop Britain signing up to the Euro, even though such a referendum is a long way off. This continual drip, drip drip of propaganda does influence voters.

Conclusion

The problem when examining voting behaviour is that such research is inexact. Between 1950 and 1970, explanations were very straight forward, as demonstrated by Pulzer's quote. However, since the 1970s there has been electoral volatility. Explanations of voting behaviour have become far more difficult. There has been a decline in the importance of class, but no other single explanation has replaced it. The list of potential explanations in Table 12.1 highlights the difficulty in attempting to explain voting behaviour. There may be specific national issues, or regional or local ones. Individual candidates might have a large personal following, or may have been imposed on a constituency. All of these may have an impact on how people vote.

Summary of key points

DEFINITION OF VOTING BEHAVIOUR

❏ How people cast their ballots

❏ Voting behaviour may be influenced by personal, social, political or other factors

THE CASE FOR CLASS AS AN EXPLANATION OF VOTING BEHAVIOUR

❏ Class is no longer the sole explanation of voting behaviour but it is a major factor

❏ Classifications of class have changed

❏ Parties target specific 'classes' of voters at election time

❏ Other factors that may explain voting behaviour are closely linked to class

THE CASE AGAINST CLASS AS AN EXPLANATION OF VOTING BEHAVIOUR

❏ Classifications of class are far too vague to be of use

❏ Other factors have gained in importance but not necessarily across the entire UK in a uniform manner

❏ Issue voting is becoming far more prominent

❏ The media has become of far greater importance in influencing voting behaviour

Further Reading

Butler, D. and Kavanagh, D.; *The British General Election of 2001* (Palgrave, 2001) (These election studies are brought out after each general election, and include data on voting behaviour)

Heath, A., Jowell, R. and Curtice, J.; *How Britain Votes* (Pergamon Press, 1985)

Internet Sites

www.crest.ox.ac.uk/

This will take you to the CREST (Centre for Research into Elections and Social Trends) homepage

CHAPTER THIRTEEN

Local Government

INTRODUCTION

Local government is often seen as a boring subject. It can be portrayed as focusing on rubbish collection and dog waste. However, this is to demean what is a very important aspect of British politics. The reality is that local government is essential to the social and economic well-being of communities throughout the country.

Local Government

A directly-elected body to serve the local community. It ensures basic services are delivered to the community and is held to account by regular local elections.

The concept of local government can be seen as dating back to late-Elizabethan times with the introduction of the Poor Laws in 1601 and 1602, or even earlier with county sheriffs. Since these times, local government has developed and evolved, while its basic premise has remained largely unchanged. The idea of local government is to ensure basic service delivery to the local community. In the 20th and 21st Centuries, these local authorities have been held to account for their actions via local elections. Thus local government is directly elected by, and directly accountable to, their local community. They are responsible for the service provision for the local community. The major service areas or functions of local government are listed in Table 13.1.

However, with regard to service provision, the role of local government has changed. During the Thatcher years, the emphasis moved from local authorities as a provider of services to that of an enabler. Rather than providing the services for the local community, local authorities have to 'enable' others to provide those same services. The local authority may be the provider of last resort. Instead, private sector organisations and voluntary bodies have been given the opportunity to provide the local services. This has been done via a number of centrally-directed policies including Compulsory

Competitive Tendering (CCT) and the deregulation of public sector monopolies. The idea was that through competition, costs would be driven down and the quality of service would improve.

Table 13.1 Main Functions of Local Government

Civil Defence
Consumer protection
Council tax collection
Development control
Economic development
Education
Highways
Housing
Libraries
Licensing
Recreation facilities
Refuse collection
Refuse disposal
Social services
Strategic planning
Street lighting
Transport

However, what is of note is that all of these changes were centrally-dictated. There was little or no consultation with local government. The perception was that central government was out to undermine or even destroy local government. While the destruction of local government has been largely avoided (at least to date), there is still the appearance of central government trying to control local government.

Is Local Government Controlled by the Centre?
The case for central control of local government

When examining central-local relations, the constitutional position is of great importance. The constitution was examined in Chapter Three, and a written and codified constitution may clarify the relationship between the different tiers of government in the UK. However, even without such codification, it is important to note that Parliament is sovereign. This means that Parliament is the supreme law making body. It can delegate powers to lesser tiers, such as local government, but it can also take these and other powers away from the lesser tiers. Ultimately, as local government was created through a series of Acts of Parliament, central government could abolish local government. Such an action has happened, with the 1985 Local Government Act, which abolished the Greater London Council (GLC) and the six Metropolitan County Councils (Manchester, Merseyside, South Yorkshire, Tyne and Wear, West Midlands, and West Yorkshire).

On top of this, from a constitutional perspective, local government is restricted in what it can do. Should a council take action beyond those stipulated by Parliament then the council will be acting *ultra vires*. This term translates as "beyond its powers". Thus, with the concept of Parliamentary sovereignty and the doctrine of *ultra vires*, from a constitutional position central government is in a position to control local government. The issue tends to be over the extent to which Parliament wishes to utilise its powers.

One of the ways in which successive governments have utilised the powers of Parliament and Parliamentary sovereignty is over the restructuring of local government. Aspects of local government in England have been restructured in every decade since the 1970s. The 1972 Local Government Act introduced tiered local authorities throughout England (and Wales) and created the six Metropolitan County Councils. As noted earlier, these Metropolitan County Councils were abolished, along with the GLC, by the 1985 Local Government Act. In 1992, the Local Government Commission was established to investigate the structures of local government in England, excluding the metropolitan areas. As a result of these investigations, since 1998 there has been a mishmash of both unitary and tiered authorities throughout England, which has been described as "a dog's breakfast" (Wilson and Game, 2002, p. 67). In 1998, there was a referendum for a directly-elected Mayor of London and a new Greater London Authority (GLA). These came into being in 2000. Other local authorities, with encouragement from central government, have also had referendums for directly-elected mayors. Thus it appears that central government is in a position to manipulate the structures of local government for the apparent benefit of central government.

While England experienced some form of consultation via the Local Government Commission in 1992, both Scotland and Wales had new structures of local government imposed upon them from the centre, with little consultation. The respective Secretaries of State for Scotland and Wales imposed unitary authorities in each country, which took effect in 1996. The only debate that appeared to take place was over the number of authorities rather than the type of structures. Since the advent of devolution in 1999, local government has come under the remit of the devolved bodies in each country.

The most obvious area of central control over local government is in the realm of finance. Most of the finance for local government comes from the centre. It was the Conservative Government under Margaret Thatcher that introduced the concept of 'capping'. This was where local government expenditure was capped at a limit decided by central government. All forms of local taxation have been capped: the rates, the Community Charge, and the Council Tax. Under Thatcher there was rate capping and poll tax (Community Charge) capping. The current Blair Government is considering imposing Council Charge capping. With each version of capping, it is further evidence of central government interfering in local affairs, and arguably attempting to control the actions of local government through limiting the funding.

It is not just through the levels of local taxation that central government has attempted to control local government, but also through the system of auditing and inspection. The inspection of local government services is nothing new. The fire service, education, policing have long been covered by various inspections. What is different, particularly under the current Blair Government, is the increased number of inspections.

> [A]ll functions of an authority are subject to inspection at least once every 5 years by either an existing special inspectorate – e.g. OFSTED, the Social Services Inspectorate, the Benefit Fraud Inspectorate – or by the Audit Commission's Best Value Inspectorate. (Wilson and Game (2002) p.339)

All of these reports are published. Where appropriate, if services are continually failing, the local authority may be stripped of such service provision. The Audit Commission's Best Value Inspection reports can be seen at *www.bestvalueinspections.gov.uk*.

What is interesting is that most people would expect the Audit Commission to be concerned with finance. Local authorities must keep meticulous accounts, for these are inspected by the Audit Commission. However, as Chandler (2001, p.68) points out:

> The Audit Commission was given greater powers than solely the duty of checking the legality of the accounts. It is also responsible for ascertaining whether local authorities are providing value for money and this has enabled the Commission to comment extensively on the management of local government.

This is not to suggest that the Audit Commission is merely an agent of central government. In fact, the Audit Commission has also been critical of the way in which central government has managed local government. Yet the standards to which local government must reach in service delivery tend to be set by the centre.

The final aspect of the way in which central government controls local government can be seen in the replacement of the concept 'local government' with local governance. This is where central government has utilised alternative bodies in the provision of local services, rather than local government. Much of this can be linked to the Thatcherite ideal of the enabling authority (mentioned earlier in this chapter). Many of these bodies now providing the services are centrally appointed. Some of them are quangos, and these bodies were examined in Chapter Eight. Miller and Dickson (2000) raised the question as to whether or not the public even cared who delivered the services. Their extensive survey found that the public liked the idea of local democracy but were happy regardless of who provided a specific service, as long as it was provided to the highest possible standard.

Miller and Dickson also found that the appointed personnel were often far less in touch with local needs and requirements than the elected councillors. Many of the appointments were not even 'local'. This highlights the extent to which the role of local government has changed. It is no longer considered a service provider but is a service enabler. Benchmarks are set by the centre. If these are met, the centre will 'reward' the council. If not, the centre may remove the particular service from the council and run it themselves. This devaluation of local government is such that many people seem unconcerned by its demise. The centre is calling the tune. Constitutionally, local government must dance to it.

The case against central control of local government

The idea that central government is able to control local government is something of an overstatement. Constitutionally at least, the centre may dominate. But to describe the relationship as one of control is to go several steps too far. Control is too strong a label. It would be more accurate to describe central government as being influential in some of the affairs of local government, providing "guidance" wherever the centre thinks it is necessary (Chandler, 2001, p.72). The idea of control is to be able to make some one do something that they would not otherwise do. There is very little that central government can do in this respect without some penalty. Even the issue of capping is fraught with danger. To compel councils to lower their council tax levies is to invite a backlash against cuts in services. Even when the rises in council tax appear excessive (as occurred in 2004), central government has appeared loathe to intervene. Central government may condemn the excessive rises but appears happier to let the voting public decide a council's future at the ballot box.

Britain is a highly centralised state. Even after the introduction of devolution for Scotland, Wales and Northern Ireland, Britain has remained centralised. Parliament remains the supreme law making body. The parameters of operation set for local government are decided by the centre – either at Whitehall or Westminster. Thereafter, local authorities have a degree of flexibility of operation within those parameters.

An important aspect of local government is that it is directly elected. Through local elections, councils and councillors are held to account for their actions. What we have here is local accountability. These elections set local government apart from all other sub-national institutions (with the exception of the devolved bodies in Scotland, Wales and Northern Ireland). They may be viewed in a similar light to national elections. Every four or five years, the voting public are given the opportunity to pass judgement on the policy record of central government, and to hold the elected personnel to account for their actions. The same applies to local authorities every four years. Thus in 2003, the people of Leicester voted out the Labour administration for the first time in over twenty years (see Table 13.2).

Table 13.2 Leicester City Council election result 2003

Party	2003 (seats won)	1999 (seats won)
Liberal Democrats	25	16
Labour	20	28
Conservative	9	9
Independent	0	3

Note: ward boundaries were redrawn for Leicester City Council prior to the 2003 local elections

Much of the local accountability is to do with service provision. If local services are being provided to an acceptable standard, and the council tax is not too high (or has not increased by too much), then a council can reasonably expect to be re-elected on its track record. This will be regardless of central government machinations.

Service provision was a key function of local authorities. As noted in the introduction to this chapter, much of this role was reduced in the 1980s as local authorities became enablers rather than providers. Today, little has changed.

However, local authorities may still be perceived as service providers or service deliverers. They are blamed if the rubbish bins are not emptied – even if it is a private contractor who is actually providing the service. Table 13.1 listed the main functions of local government – the services that are provided. There is an obligation on local authorities to ensure that these services are provided – although councils may not provide the actual services. Thus they are held to account for the service provision: for the contracts negotiated with the private or voluntary organisations, and the monitoring of the service provision. The centre may have set the parameters by which local authorities operate in service provision, but it is the authorities who are held to account for that provision.

Another reason why central government does not control local government can be presented at the level of semantics. There is no single 'local government'. Rather, throughout the UK there are 467 elected local governments. Each local government (or council) has its own special needs and requirements. Is it feasible to lump the requirements of Rutland, Cardiff and the Highlands together? They may all be unitary authorities (a single tier of government) but the actual demands placed upon each council by the respective local communities are significantly different.

Only since May 2005 has there been a uniform central government position on local government. The Minister for Communities and Local Government is currently held by David Miliband. This is not the only government department that deals with local government. The website *www.info4local.gov.uk*, which provides local authorities with a vast quantity of information, is run by six other government departments, with other departments and agencies making a contribution. The six departments are:

Office of Deputy Prime Minister
Education and Skills
Health
Home Office
Transport
Work and Pensions

While this shows some co-ordination between government departments in the provision of information for local authorities, it does not mean that all government departments will treat local authorities in a similar fashion. Even within these departments, one local authority may be treated in a different manner to another.

The whole debate over the central control of local government obscures a far more important debate on the role of local government. Although Britain is still a highly centralised state, we are now seeing the creation of multiple tiers of government and a transformation to multi-level governance. This shift from government to governance has been instigated by the centre. It sees the downplaying of elected local government and, in some areas, its replacement with indirectly elected or unelected bodies. According to Wilson and Game (2002, p.18), local governance "more effectively describes the extensive network of public, voluntary and private sector bodies that are nowadays involved in policy-making and service delivery at the sub-central level". The idea is that there is a partnership between several different bodies to enable the best possible service provision. There is interaction between the different partners. It is not necessarily a case of government (central or local) dominating. Individual local councils have become one of a number of actors involved in local governance. Businesses, quangos and voluntary organisations are all now involved in some aspects of local service provision.

The problem here is accountability. As John and Cole (2000, p.87) ask: "Who governs governance?" The whole system of governance has become so complex that it is now very difficult to know who is making the decisions. Decision making takes place behind closed doors. This may in itself undermine accountability. As the number of actors involved in local governance grows, the ability of central government (or anybody else for that matter) to control local government diminishes.

Conclusion

The whole issue of the extent to which central government controls local government is complicated. The relationship between the two is often fraught with difficulties. The idea of the centre 'controlling' local government is possibly going too far. However, central government does have great influence over local government, and does wield power over local government as well. The parameters by which local government can operate are set by central government. The extent of this can be seen in the Charnwood District Council's Local Development Framework (May 2004, p.3):

> We will need to reflect planning guidance laid down at national, regional and County level. This establishes a broad context to guide the approach the Council can take locally... We cannot depart from this framework.
>
> *(www.charnwood.gov.uk/uploads/10838369179765.pdf)*

Thus the parameters are set by higher tiers of government, particularly the centre, as to what (in this particular case) Charnwood District Council can do as part of their development plan. All councils in England will be working under similar constraints.

Yet the whole idea of central government controlling local government actually hides a far more important issue – the transformation from local government to local governance. Local government has been compelled to draw in private organisations and voluntary bodies into the policy formulation process as well as the implementation process – which can be seen in the various Local Development Frameworks across England. This use of quangos can be seen as undermining local democracy. The issue of quangos enhancing or undermining democracy was addressed in Chapter Eight. However, it raises the question of what is the role of local government? With local election turnouts falling, there appears to be little interest in what local government does. And as the transformation to governance continues, the role of local government appears to be diminishing. It is highly unlikely that central government will abolish local government. They may appear to be influencing what local government can do, but it also appears as if central government is letting local government wither and die.

Summary of key points

DEFINITION OF LOCAL GOVERNMENT

◻   A body that is elected by the local community, accountable to the local community and is responsible for the delivery of services to the local community.

THE CASE FOR CENTRAL CONTROL OF LOCAL GOVERNMENT

◻   The constitutional relationship is of great importance. The centre (Parliament) remains sovereign. It can delegate powers, or rescind them. The constitutional relationship is of great importance. The centre (Parliament) remains sovereign. It can delegate powers, or rescind them.

◻   If local government acts beyond those powers delegated to it, it will be deemed to be acting *ultra vires* (beyond its powers)

◻   The centre restructures local government on a regular basis

◻   The centre controls the purse strings

◻   The centre has changed the role of local government from a service provider to a service enabler

◻   Unelected bodies are carrying out tasks formerly carried out by local authorities

THE CASE AGAINST CENTRAL CONTROL OF LOCAL GOVERNMENT

❏ The centre dominates centre-local relations, but it can not 'control' local government – it is too strong a label

❏ There is flexibility for local government within the powers delegated from the centre

❏ Local government is elected and is accountable to the local community

❏ There is no single local government – there are 467 councils in the UK

❏ More and more actors are involved in local governance of which local government is but one

Further Reading

Chandler, J.; *Local Government Today* (Manchester University Press, 2001, 3rd edition)

John, P. and Cole, A.; "Policy Networks and Local Political Leadership in Britain and France" in Stoker, G. (ed.); *The New Politics of British Local Governance* (Macmillan, 2000)

Loughlin, M.; "The Constitutional Status of Local Government" in Pratchett, L. and Wilson, D. (eds.); *Local Democracy and Local Government* (Macmillan, 1996)

Miller, B. and Dickson, M.; "Local Governance: The Assessments of Councillors, Quango Members and the Public" in Stoker, G. (ed.); *The New Politics of British Local Governance* (Macmillan, 2000)

Pratchett, L. and Wilson, D. (eds.); *Local Democracy and Local Government* (Macmillan, 1996)

Stoker, G. (ed.); *The New Politics of British Local Governance* (Macmillan, 2000)

Wilson, D.; "Unravelling control freakery: redefining central-local government relations" *British Journal of Politics and International Relations* vol. 4, 2003

Wilson, D. and Game C.; *Local Government in the United Kingdom* (Palgrave, 2002, 3rd edition)

Internet Sites

www.bestvalueinspections.gov.uk

The Audit Commission's Best Value web page

www.info4local.gov.uk

A useful guide for local authorities to find information on central government websites

www.odpm.gov.uk

Office of the Deputy Prime Minister home page

CHAPTER FOURTEEN
Devolution and Regionalism

INTRODUCTION

Since the election of the Labour Government in 1997, great steps have been taken in decentralising British politics. Scotland, Wales and Northern Ireland each have their own directly elected devolved bodies – a parliament in Scotland and assemblies in Northern Ireland and Wales. It was hoped that such a step would rejuvenate the political arenas in each country, and with a possible knock on effect of creating demand for regional assemblies in England. This was the political aspect of devolution.

Devolution

The transfer of power from central government to a lower tier. This lower tier of government ought to be elected and accountable to the people. However, administrative devolution focuses upon service delivery at a regional level without electoral accountability for the region.

Bogdanor (1999, p.2) has defined devolution as "the transfer to a subordinate elected body on a geographical basis, of functions at present exercised by ministers and Parliament". These functions could be legislative (making laws) or executive (implementing the decisions made by a superior body). At all times, Westminster remains sovereign. Thus the Scottish Parliament has been given clear legislative powers, including the right to raise or lower income tax by up to three pence (although the Scotland Act (1998) was more precise on the reserved powers of Westminster than the powers of the Scottish Parliament). The Welsh and Northern Ireland Assemblies were given some legislative powers but within rigorous frameworks. A brief overview of the key powers is presented in Table 14.1.

Table 14.1 Key powers of the devolved bodies in Scotland, Wales and Northern Ireland

Scotland	Wales	Northern Ireland
Can make primary legislation in a range of areas, including:	Can develop and implement policies in a range of areas, including:	Can make primary legislation in a range of areas, including:
Education	Agriculture	Agriculture and rural development
Environment	Culture	Culture, arts and leisure
Fire services	Education and training	Education
Health	Health and health services	Enterprise, trade and investment
Justice	Housing	Environment
Local government	Local government	Health and social services
Police	Social services	Regional development
Rural affairs	Transport and roads	Social development
Social work	Welsh language	
Tax-varying powers		All decisions to be taken on a cross-community basis.
Transport		

Primary legislation – any legislation that is not reserved by Westminster can be passed (subject to the Human Rights Act and membership of the EU)

Secondary legislation – the broad outline of legislation is made by Parliament but the detail as to how it is implemented is left to the sub-ordinate body

Yet these great strides actually mask a significant aspect of British politics. The referendums that led to devolution were not the first moves in breaking up the centralised state of Britain. Administrative devolution has been around for well over a century, and is not really encapsulated in the Bogdanor definition of devolution cited above. The Scottish Office was created in 1885, with similar Offices set up for Wales (1964) and Northern Ireland (1972). Added to this, the civil service has also been devolved. Not all civil servants are based in Whitehall. They have been dispersed around the country, not just in the territorial Offices of Scotland, Wales and Northern Ireland, but in other departments as well. For example, there is deconcentration of the civil service, with the Inland Revenue headquarters being relocated to Nottingham. There is also decentralisation, with some policy-making powers being handed down to local government.

On top of all this, there are already regional bodies operating within England. Again, these do not fit the Bogdanor definition of devolution because they are not elected at this moment in time. There are Regional Development Agencies covering all of England. Although unelected, these quangos (see Chapter Eight) have had significant powers given to them by central government, in particular focusing upon economic development and regeneration. The RDAs may be the precursor for directly elected regional government in Britain. If such moves go ahead (and regional referendums were planned for 2004 in the Northeast of England), this could be perceived as a stepping stone towards the development of a federal Britain.

Are we moving towards a federal Britain?

The case for Britain becoming federal

Arguments for the development of a federal Britain can be presented from both ends of the spectrum. Firstly, it can be a means to prevent the break up of the United Kingdom. Secondly, there are arguments about further formalising and strengthening the powers that have been devolved, possibly via constitutional reform. What currently exists in the UK is, in effect, a quasi-federal system, with different parts of the country able to wield different powers.

In the 1970s, Tam Dalyell argued that devolution would lead to the break up of the UK. His book, *Devolution: The End of Britain* (1977), presented a range of points which highlighted many of the potential problems that would arise with the introduction of devolution. Dalyell envisaged similar problems in Scotland as to those which existed in Northern Ireland, with many Scots actually using devolution as a stepping stone to demand independence. To date, such a bleak outlook has not been realised. However, the formalisation of the devolution, by integrating it into the constitution may prevent Dalyell's nightmare vision from happening.

There is a fear that Parliament may, at some time in the future, reverse the devolution legislation. The Conservative Party presents itself as the party of the Union. Devolution can be seen as a challenge to the Union, thus a future Conservative Government may act accordingly. At this moment in time, such an action is not envisaged. This is not to say that it will never occur. However, in reversing the devolution legislation, Dalyell's scenario of a second Northern Ireland (with all the terrorism that has occurred over the past decades) may actually happen. To prevent the possibility of such a situation, the formalisation of devolution in the constitution may be the way forward.

By invoking such a constitutional change, devolution would become a form of federalism by default. Under devolution, devolved powers can be returned to the centre. In a federal structure, the division of power is protected by the constitution. By enshrining the devolved powers in the constitution, Britain would be recreating itself as a federal state. Bogdanor (2003, p. 28) has described the relationship between the Scottish Parliament and Westminster as "quasi-federal". He argues that there is not simply a delegation of powers, but rather a division of power to legislate. To protect and develop this relationship, and even to extend it to the remainder of the country, there is a need for a rethink over the constitution.

Such a move would formalise and protect the devolved parts of Britain. However, such a move may actually lead to greater demands for powers to be transferred from the centre to the regions. Currently, Scotland, Wales and Northern Ireland all have different levels of power devolved to their elected bodies. The creation of a federal Britain could actually bring uniformity to the powers that have been devolved. Such a move would mean increased powers to Wales and Northern Ireland, but may mean a reduction in some of the powers transferred to the Scottish Parliament. The most likely power to be transferred would be the ability to vary levels of income tax.

One question that would arise would be the role of England. Within the current structure, England dominates, being far larger than the other component parts of the UK. Under a federal structure, England would probably be divided into regions to prevent such domination from continuing. It would bring directly elected regional government to all of England, bringing a uniformity of governance to all of the UK. This could happen via devolution. However, as noted above, protecting such development via constitutional reform would mean the formation of federal structures.

There is some debate in parts of England about devolution. The North East and the South West of England have both seen the experiences in Scotland and Wales respectively. A simple question has arisen: "Why not us?" School children are being sent across the border into Scotland to benefit from the Scottish education system, where class sizes are smaller and teachers better paid and consequently better motivated. There are no university tuition fees for Scottish students, and the Welsh Assembly is demanding the power to implement similar legislation. Once parts of England gain directly elected regional government, devolution will probably be implemented across all of England – if nothing else, for the sake of consistency across the country.

A small point about devolution is that there remains dependence upon the centre – via funding. Thus any change to policies, such as increasing the pay of teachers in Scotland above the national norm, is at the expense of other policies. A block of money is handed over to the devolved bodies to spend as they see fit (within the parameters of their given powers). So, although there are a number of powers wielded by the various devolved bodies (as listed in Table 14.1), there is still significant overlap of responsibilities with Westminster

(Mitchell, 2003). Under a federal system, greater flexibility may well exist, reducing much of the dependence on the centre.

The creation of a federal Britain could also strengthen local government. Currently, the role of local government can be changed by the whim of Parliament (see Chapter Thirteen). Powers can be given and removed from local government; local government can be restructured by the centre without consultation. A federal structure would actually protect local government. As with all tiers of government under a federal structure, the role and powers of local government would be protected.

The case against Britain becoming federal

Currently, Britain has a unitary constitution. This means that there is a single source of power – Parliament, or the Queen-in-Parliament to be precise. It is Parliament which can devolve powers, but such a decision can also be reversed by Parliament. Thus Parliament can grant powers to local authorities, or establish devolved bodies. As Parliament cannot bind its' successors, any of these decisions may be repealed.

A federal system, on the other hand, establishes a range of different power bases. It would be a fundamental change that would undermine the traditions of British history as well as undermining the British Parliament. Rather than Parliament being able to legislate for the country collectively, it would be prevented from legislating in particular fields. In the United States, for example, capital punishment, and regulatory powers over industry, business and public utilities are all wielded by state governments. Thus not all states have the same laws. Offences that are punishable by death in one state may not be so harshly treated in another. Potentially, this may make government very complicated.

The devolved powers that have been given to Scotland, Wales and Northern Ireland are dissimilar. Added to this there is also the administrative devolution in England. This can be described as asymmetric devolution (Bogdanor, 2003). Yet Britain is not the only country in Europe to have such a set up. Spain adopted a devolved system in their 1978 constitution. This created seventeen autonomous regions. Although they are funded from the centre, they have powers to adopt a separate line from central government. Spain has "a high degree of regional autonomy, yet falling short of a fully federal system" (Gallagher, Laver and Mair, 1995, p. 148). Some regions, including Catalonia, Galicia and Andalucia, have greater levels of autonomy than their counterparts across the rest of Spain. The specific powers that have been devolved are clearly outlined (see Table 14.2), but it was up to each region as to how much of this devolved power they wished to take. Even the development of devolution is left to the regions rather than being pushed or controlled by the centre. This system appears to be working very well in Spain, and there is no reason why the same cannot occur in Britain. If anything, it is the 'hands off' approach adopted by the Spanish central government that appears to encourage the success of devolution.

Table 14.2 Powers of the Autonomous Regions of Spain

The Spanish constitution provides certain powers for the autonomous regions. These include:

Agriculture

Culture

Economic development

Environmental protection

Forestry

Housing

Internal organisation of regional government

Planning

Social assistance

Source: www.rpani.gov.uk/studyvisit/spain.htm

A related problem for any moves towards a federal system is the role of local government. Currently, there are two tiers of elected government in England (although some parts of England have two tiers of local government), and three in Scotland, Wales and Northern Ireland. On top of this there is also the European Union. Regardless of having a devolved system or a federal one, the structures of government are already too complicated. In Scotland and Wales the devolved bodies have been granted powers from local government as well as from the centre. A federal system would not necessarily clarify the roles of the various tiers of government. To use the USA as an example, while there are reserved powers for the federal government (such as defence and foreign affairs), others were left for local jurisdictions (e.g. education). In the case of education, most funding is provided by state and local government. The federal government provides about 5% of funding. The problem is whether education is a local issue or a state issue, as well as questioning whether the federal funding has any strings attached.

With so many tiers of government, be it under a federal or a devolved system of government, withdrawal of participation by the public becomes commonplace. In the elections to the devolved bodies in Scotland and Wales in 2003, the turnout was 49.4% and 38.2% respectively. The turnout for US elections is also exceedingly low (50.4% in the 2000 Presidential election, with other tiers of government far lower). Too many tiers of government may appear too complicated for the average member of the public. Consequently, participation levels drop. It is not simply a case of preventing a federal structure being imposed on Britain. Rather, it may be a case of eliminating at least one tier of government.

Conclusion

Each part of the United Kingdom is currently governed in a different way. Scotland, Wales and Northern Ireland each have a directly elected tier of government for their own country. Each of these has different powers. England has an unelected tier of regional bodies – Regional Development Agencies. While this lack of uniformity appears problematic (at least to students of British politics), it does not mean that such a system does not work efficiently. Spain has used this system of asymmetric devolution since 1978 with few problems.

The issue is more to do with how to protect the devolved bodies. As Parliament is the supreme law making body, it would be possible for a future Parliament to repeal the devolution legislation. Even allowing for the complicated situation in Northern Ireland, the devolved assembly there has been suspended on several occasions with powers returned to Westminster. A future Conservative Government could repeal all the devolution legislation – the question would be at what cost?

To prevent any such action, a change to the constitution would be required. This would protect the devolved bodies. A move to a federal system would most likely require uniformity of powers to all devolved areas – Scotland, Wales, Northern Ireland and the English regions. It is not so clear cut as to whether any part of the United Kingdom would want to accept such a move.

Summary of key points
DEFINITION OF DEVOLUTION
❐ The transfer of powers from central government to a lower tier of government

❐ Political devolution would involve the new tier of government to be directly elected

❐ Administrative devolution does not require the electoral element

THE CASE FOR BRITAIN BECOMING FEDERAL

☐ Devolution could be seen as the first step towards the break up of the UK. A federal structure could prevent that from happening

☐ Devolution can be reversed by any future Westminster Parliament. A federal structure would prevent that from happening

☐ A federal structure would strengthen all tiers of government, and protect them from a potentially dominant centre

THE CASE AGAINST BRITAIN BECOMING FEDERAL

☐ A federal system would undermine Parliamentary sovereignty

☐ Asymmetric devolution exists at the moment. A federal structure would mean some devolved bodies ceding powers back to the centre

☐ With so many tiers of government, withdrawal of public participation becomes commonplace

Further Reading

Bogdanor, V.; *Devolution in the United Kingdom* (Oxford University Press, 1999)

Bogdanor, V.; "Asymmetric Devolution: Towards a Quasi-Federal Constitution" in Dunleavy, P., Gamble, A., Heffernan, R. and Peele, G. (eds.); *Developments in British Politics* 7 (Palgrave, 2003)

Dalyell, T.; *Devolution: The End of Britain* (Jonathon Cape, 1977)

Gallagher, M., Laver, M. and Mair, P.; *Representative Government in Modern Europe* (McGraw-Hill, 1995, 2nd edition)

Mitchell, J.; "Politics in Scotland" in Dunleavy, P., Gamble, A., Heffernan, R. and Peele, G. (eds.); *Developments in British Politics* 7 (Palgrave, 2003)

Internet Sites

www.ni-assembly.gov.uk

Northern Ireland Assembly homepage

www.northernireland.gov.uk

Homepage of the Northern Ireland Executive

www.rpani.gov.uk/studyvisit/spain.htm

Review of Public Administration study visit to Spain, detailing the structures of Spanish Government *www.scotland.gov.uk*

Homepage of the Scottish Executive

www.scottish.parliament.uk

Scottish Parliament homepage

www.wales.gov.uk/index.htm

Homepage of the National Assembly for Wales

CHAPTER FIFTEEN

Britain and the European Union

INTRODUCTION

The relationship between Britain and the European Union (EU) is extremely complicated. When the original bodies were formed in the 1950s (the European Coal and Steel Community (ECSC) and the European Economic Community (EEC)), Britain refused to participate. Reasons for non-participation included Britain's perceived global role, the nationalisation of coal, steel and other industries, and the special relationship with the USA. However, the success of the EEC was such that Britain tried to set up an organisation to counter it (the European Free Trade Association or EFTA). The lack of success in EFTA was such that Britain applied to join the EEC in 1961, and again in 1967, before finally being accepted in 1971. On 1 January 1973, Britain joined the EEC.

> ### European Union
>
> A body whose origins lie in the European Coal and Steel Community and the European Economic Community. Britain joined what was then called the EEC in 1973. Currently there are 25 member states. There is debate as to whether the EU is simply a trading bloc or a stepping stone towards a fully integrated, federal Europe.

Upon joining, it would be expected that a new member state would wish to acquiesce to the methods of operation that have been utilised in the past – but not Britain. The terms of entry were renegotiated, and a referendum was held on continued membership; all within eighteen months of joining. Even after this, one particular prime minister in a handbagging mood demanded "our" money back. It is unsurprising that Britain earned the label "reluctant European". If anything, the label was in greater use after joining than beforehand.

The problem is that the term "reluctant European" has no clear definition. At a basic level, the concept suggests that Britain does not want to remain in the EU. Very few people follow this vein. Rather, there appears to be dissatisfaction with Europe: the idea that unelected bureaucrats in Brussels are ruling our lives, compelling the British people to use metric measurements, banning the British sausage, and making our lives generally unbearable. Much of this is actually a myth, but it is one that is pedalled by large parts of the British tabloid press. Headlines such as "Up Yours, Delors", as well as mythical stories of donkeys having to wear nappies on the beach, have created a rather xenophobic attitude towards Europe.

Thus the idea of Britain as a reluctant European may actually stem from a lack of knowledge about the role of the EU in our lives. It cannot be disputed that EU law takes precedence over British law when the two conflict (see Chapter Three on the Constitution). Yet there have been many benefits from British membership. The problem is that these stories are often deemed un-newsworthy. After all, bad news makes news, and the EU is a very easy target to hit. Hence there is a perception of Britain a reluctant European.

Is Britain still the 'reluctant' European?

The case for Britain as the reluctant European

Much of the perception of British reluctance towards Europe may stem from the early post-war years. Britain had won the war, and the future looked rosy. Winston Churchill spoke of the formation of a United States of Europe, with all the European states working together under the supervision of the superpowers – USA, USSR and Britain. The Europeans all lost in the war. Britain had been the bulwark against Nazism, and had emerged victorious. Britain was 'better' than the other Europeans, and did not need to join in any of their rebuilding schemes. There was no way in which Britain would want to join a 'losers' club.

Added to this Britain had a 'special relationship' with the USA. This relationship developed during the war and into the Cold War against communism. The ties of language, in particular, drew Britain closer to the USA. This relationship has been perceived by successive British governments as the corner stone of all defence policies. The USA dominates the North Atlantic Treaty Organisation (NATO). Even today, the links with the USA and NATO appear to supersede everything else. This was notable in the debate over Iraq. Britain stood by the USA against the position of most of her EU counterparts. There is this mentality that the USA knows best, and that the EU ought to look more to the USA.

A third strand of reluctance stems from the perception that Britain still has an obligation to look after the old Empire. Thus, Britain wants to be able to trade with the Commonwealth rather than with the EU. Even during the negotiations in the early 1970s, there was much consternation over the future of imports of butter and lamb from New Zealand (see Uwe Kitzinger; *Diplomacy and Persuasion* (1973) for an excellent analysis of the protracted negotiations over membership). The obligations of Empire (or, more accurately, Commonwealth) remained during the negotiations and beyond. Even today, there are some Conservative MPs who look to the Commonwealth as an alternative source of trade to the EU.

In the 1960s, General de Gaulle refused to allow Britain to join the EEC because he felt that it would allow the USA to intervene in European affairs via the back door. Britain would be a Trojan horse that would allow American influence into the EEC (arguably to undermine the dominant French position). De Gaulle felt that Britain was not committed to the EEC vision, and would always look to America first.

Even looking from inside the EU, Britain appears reluctant. In the 1980s, Margaret Thatcher argued that Britain paid too much into the European budget, and demanded a rebate. This rebate has become sacrosanct. According to successive British Governments, it is non-negotiable. Even when examining the future enlargement of the EU in 2004, and how to fund this enlargement, the British position was that the rebate could not be touched. Other sources of funding the enlargement had to be examined instead – especially the Common Agricultural Policy. Britain's attitude is that British interests come first, even if it is at the expense of the EU.

Another feature of Britain's reluctant membership has been to negotiate opt outs of any policies that do not appeal to the British people. The obvious example has been over joining the euro. In the negotiations on the Treaty of European Union (TEU) at Maastricht, John Major negotiated a number of opt outs. These included the single currency and the Social Charter. The position on the Social Charter was reversed by Tony Blair in 1997. However, with regard to the single currency, a number of hurdles have been set by Gordon Brown and Tony Blair. There will be a referendum on joining the Euro when Britain passes the five economic 'tests' set by the Treasury. These can be seen in Table 15.1.

These tests were evaluated in June 2003. Gordon Brown effectively announced that only one test had been passed (financial services). Steps were needed to be taken by both Britain and the EU to enable all of the tests to be achieved. Even though the Euro is up and running (relatively successfully), the British Government expects the EU to make some alterations to enable Britain to join. No other member has been so audacious or impudent.

Table 15.1 The Five Economic 'Tests' for joining the Euro

> Would joining Economic and Monetary Union (EMU) create better conditions for firms making long term decisions to invest in the UK?
>
> How would adopting the single currency affect Britain's financial services?
>
> Are business cycles and economic structures compatible so that we and others in Europe could live comfortably with Euro interest rates on a permanent basis?
>
> If problems emerge, is there sufficient flexibility to deal with them?
>
> Will joining EMU help to promote growth, stability and a lasting increase in jobs?

Yet it is not just over the Euro that Britain is reluctant. The draft European constitution, drawn up by Valerie Giscard d'Estaing has drawn an enormous amount of flack in the British press. It has been portrayed as the end of the British constitution. While this draft constitution is little more than a codification of EU laws that already exist, a number of British newspapers – most prominent was the Daily Mail – demanded a referendum on whether or not Britain should accept this constitution. The Daily Mail ran its own 'referendum' on 12 June 2003 to demand such a referendum, even though no such document existed at that time. The Mail's 'referendum' was described as "totally flawed" (*Guardian* 13 June 2003) due to, among other things, the lack of impartial information provided by the newspaper and the opportunity for voters to cast multiple votes. The Daily Mail is vitriolic in its opposition to anything to do with the EU and its' readership unsurprisingly demanded a referendum to be able to oppose the proposed constitution.

While the British Government appeared a little enthusiastic about Giscard d'Estaing's proposals, there was a caveat. The word 'federal' was removed from the draft treaty. This was presented as a huge triumph for Britain, as it would mean that a European superstate could not be created. There was a similar situation during the debate over the TEU in 1991, where John Major was also able to get the word 'federal' removed from the Treaty. There appears to be a huge fixation over this concept. The word federal is equated with a European superstate and that would be the end of a thousand years of history, and the end of Britain as we know it.

Put bluntly, there is a fear – or possibly paranoia – in Britain of a single Europe. This applies to the political concept. Economically, Britain appears quite happy to participate in a single Europe. Thus a single market with no internal barriers to trade is considered to be acceptable. Even a fortress Europe mentality about trade with non-EU members appears to be acceptable. The economics and the trade appear largely unproblematic. Yet when concepts such as federalism arise, there is consternation. In 1988, Margaret Thatcher made a speech in Bruges where she supported a free market economy for Europe, but adamantly opposed any forms of political integration. She drew parallels with the way in which the USSR was run, inferring that a similar situation would appear in Europe. Member states were important for what they were, and should remain so. This position is still quite strong in the Conservative Party today, although more and more MPs appear to be adopting a stronger line against any involvement in Europe.

There is a fear that greater involvement in the EU will lead to the demise of Britain. Such a perspective is presented in papers such as the Sun, the Telegraph and the Daily Mail. The counter-arguments are not covered by these papers, nor are they presented by the government. Consequently, Britain appears to be not only a reluctant European, but one that is getting more and more paranoid about the EU. This was well demonstrated by Robert Kilroy Silk and other candidates of the UK Independence Party during the 2004 elections to the European Parliament. They rubbished the EU. Kilroy Silk even promised that if elected he would not take up his seat, or that if he did he would work to make the European Parliament fail. Throughout the entire election campaign, it appeared as if many UKIP candidates had little understanding as to the role of the EU in Britain today. From the UKIP perspective, most Britons are not reluctant Europeans but rather want out of Europe altogether.

The case against Britain as the reluctant European

Britain may have been a reluctant European during the formation of both the European Coal and Steel Community and the EEC, but since joining the label has become inappropriate. It took time for Britain to join. Even in the 1950s, the founding father of the EU, Jean Monnet, pointed out that: "We will have to build Europe without you [Britain]: but then you will come in and join us". The future for Britain was in Europe, not outside. Thus, apart from General de Gaulle, most European leaders wanted Britain to participate. It was only as successive British Governments came to realise the extent to which Britain's role in the world had diminished that they looked to Europe. It may have been reluctantly, but Britain did eventually join.

The perception of British reluctance has come from a range of sources, most notably the media. The role of the EU is often oversimplified in the press. The EU is considered a soft target, one incapable of fighting back. It is very rare for the media to publish good news stories from the EU, such as the development of the riverfront in Newcastle or the construction of the A55 across North Wales. The EU also contributes towards the running of a number of agricultural courses in Britain (up to 75% of the costs). Thus, for example, courses on training in alpaca management and alpaca husbandry are available for either farmers wishing to diversify or for newcomers wishing to own or breed alpacas. Yet such support is not publicised very widely. It is far easier to talk about banning the British sausage or fishermen to wear hair nets (again both unfounded stories) than to highlight any benefits EU membership actually brings to the UK.

It would actually be fair to point out that Britain has been to the forefront in attempting to reform certain aspects of the EU. This has been most noticeable over the Common Agricultural Policy (CAP), but also over the European Parliament and the Commission. This position has been quite public under the Blair Government, but was also a feature of the Major Government. For example, whereas Margaret Thatcher went into negotiations prepared to oppose anything; both Major and Blair have entered into negotiations with their own wish lists, as well as areas about which they were unenthusiastic. Major entered the Maastricht Treaty negotiations wanting the creation of an ombudsman for the European Parliament; the application of subsidiarity in health and education; the creation of a common foreign and security policy (admittedly outside of the TEU, subject to unanimous decision making and without undermining NATO). He was opposed to the word 'federal', and was reluctant to cede too many powers to the European Parliament. Blair has pushed for an elected President of the EU and has been very enthusiastic about enlargement. He has even been supportive of the draft EU constitution drawn up by Valerie Giscard d'Estaing, although as noted earlier in this chapter, Blair was also opposed to the word 'federal'.

On the CAP, the reluctant Europeans appear to be the French, Spanish and Irish. All three states have been very reluctant to reform the CAP because of the huge subsidies that their agricultural sectors receive. With the enlargement of the EU in 2004, and ten new member states all demanding farming subsidies, the EU will not be able to pay out. Thus reform of the CAP is essential. Britain has been pushing for such reforms for a very long time and with some success as some reforms will take place from 2005. Of these, the most prominent change to the CAP is the way in which subsidies are allocated. Originally, the emphasis was upon output − the more farmers produced the more money they received. The original plan behind the CAP was to make Europe self-sufficient in food production. It has been a remarkably successful policy − possibly too successful as it has led to overproduction and excesses of a range of products, including butter, wine, olive oil and wheat. From 2005, farmers will get a single flat rate handout in relation to the size of their farm – although the French, Spanish and Irish have all negotiated deals to postpone these changes until 2007.

Under the Blair Government, but also under that of Major, Britain became more enthusiastic about Europe. Britain also became more pro-active in its relationship. There is now an appearance of Britain working with the EU rather than fighting it. The British may whinge about the way in which the EU interferes in their lives (for example over the use of metric weights rather than imperial) but they accept the decisions and get on with their lives. This may be part of the British political culture (see Chapter Two).

In Table 15.2, the rates of implementation of EU directives are listed by member states. While Britain sank in the league table, from 7th to 14th between 2000 and 2001, the implementation rate was still very high at over 96%. Countries such as Italy and Ireland have had special drives to improve their implementation rates, which have bolstered their league positions. Britain has not bothered with such an artificial approach. After such a drive is over, countries are likely to sink back down the league table. In the cases of Italy and Ireland, the drive to improve their implementation rates was due, in no small part, to their impending turn in holding the EU Presidency.

The basic problem for Britain is the future of the EU. This tends to be portrayed as moving in one of two directions: wider, as in a larger membership, or deeper, as in greater integration. There is considerable opposition to any movement towards a federal Europe. This is perceived as travelling too far and too fast. It would mean the end of the individual states of Europe. This may indeed be the future of the EU, but not yet. The problem is that Britain is very enthusiastic about increased trade with the EU, especially as there are no internal frontiers for the movement of goods and services within the EU. Greater economic integration appears palatable. Even the use of the Euro may be acceptable in the not too distant future. The political aspects appear not. A common interest rate may be used across the EU but not common forms of taxation.

Conversely, Britain appears enthusiastic about enlarging the EU. Again, the emphasis appears very much upon the economic benefits – the increased number of countries within the single market. Thus Britain appears enthusiastic about possible EU membership for Turkey – although other member states are less so. However, the countries that join the EU must have economies that are strong enough to add to the EU rather than being dependent upon EU subsidies to survive. Thus the likes of Bulgaria and Romania are not yet able to join the EU as they have not met all of the economic criteria.

Table 15.2 Implementation of EU directives by member states

Country	% Directives being implemented (2001)	% Directives being implemented (2000)	Ranking in 2001 (2000)
Denmark	99.26	98.46	1 (1)
Spain	98.51	97.99	2 (2)
Sweden	98.45	97.45	3 (5)
France	98.25	97.66	4 (4)
Italy	97.64	95.65	5 (13)
Netherlands	97.44	96.66	6 (8)
Luxembourg	97.36	96.18	7 (10)
Ireland	97.29	95.90	8 (11)
Belgium	97.24	97.86	9 (3)
Portugal	97.17	95.72	10 (12)
Germany	96.84	96.86	11 (6)
France	96.77	95.05	12 (14)
Greece	96.62	93.95	13 (15)
United Kingdom	**96.36**	**96.85**	**14 (7)**
Austria	95.95	96.58	15 (9)
EU 15	97.41	96.59	-

Source: *europa.eu.int/eur-lex/en/com/rpt/2002/act0324en01/1.pdf*

Commission of the European Communities; Nineteenth Annual Report on Monitoring the Application of Community Law (2001) (COM (2002) 324final)

So Britain is one of several member states that highlight the importance of the individual states as well as the collective body. However, successive British Governments have been wary of surrendering too many powers to the collective body. Rather, there is a desire for all of the component parts to work together, rather than being directed from the centre.

Conclusion

In examining the issue of Britain as a reluctant European, there are a number of quandaries. Firstly, is the focus on the present or the past (and in the case of the past, pre- or post-membership). Secondly, is the emphasis upon a commitment to greater integration or to further enlargement? The way in which these to questions are addressed will give some indication as to the extent of Britain's reluctance.

Added to this, there is also the role of the media in oversimplifying the issue of Europe. This was best demonstrated in a comment by Bill Cash (MP for Stone) at the time of the debate on the Treaty of European Union. "We are told that the choice is between accepting Maastricht or repudiating the European Community as a whole. To be anti-Maastricht is said to be anti-European." (Cash, 1992, p.14). Cash was opposed to the TEU but this did not mean that he opposed British membership of the European Community. However, for many in the media such a position was far too difficult to convey. Even today, opposition to Britain joining the Euro is equated with being anti-European.

As for the British Government, the label 'reluctant' may not be appropriate. Rather, Britain is more of a cautious European. Successive British Governments have questioned the need for greater integration, and may have acted as a brake on the EU travelling too quickly down the integrationist road. However, Britain also has a tendency to look to the USA rather than Europe. The trans-Atlantic perspective is often portrayed as being closer to Britain than that of Europe. This may not be wholly accurate (see Hutton, 2002).

A better way in which to describe Britain's relationship with the EU would be as a cautious European. For the most part, there is a commitment to remain in the EU and to participate fully in most aspects. However, greater convergence between Britain and the EU will take time and ought not to be rushed too much. It is more a matter of getting the British people used to the idea of being Europeans before hurtling towards any form of European super state.

Summary of key points

DEFINITION OF A RELUCTANT EUROPEAN

❏ This term is very difficult to define as there are a number of different perspectives

❏ Some people wish for Britain to withdraw from the EU

❏ Some reluctant Europeans want a commitment to no further EU integration

❏ Some reluctant Europeans want the EU to be a trading bloc, and that Britain should reclaim her sovereignty

THE CASE FOR BRITAIN BEING A RELUCTANT EUROPEAN

❏ Britain did not join in during the formative years, but joined as a last resort

❏ The 'special relationship' with the USA

❏ Obligations to the Commonwealth

❏ Thatcher demanding 'our' money back, and subsequent governments adopting a similar attitude towards EU finances

❏ Refusal to join the Euro, as well as other 'opt outs'

THE CASE AGAINST BRITAIN BEING A RELUCTANT EUROPEAN

❏ No agreement on the term 'reluctant European'. The vast majority of the British population accept EU membership, even if they do not like it

❏ Britain has been to the forefront in fighting corruption in the EU

❏ Successive British governments have been keen to enlarge the EU

❏ Britain has been keen to modernise the EU, politically, economically and socially

❏ British governments have questioned some EU proposals. Such questioning is portrayed as reluctance whereas such questioning often improves the policies

Further Reading

Cash, W.; Europe: *The Crunch* (Duckworth, 1992)

Hutton, W.; *The World We're In* (Little Brown, 2002)

Kitzinger, U.; *Diplomacy and Persuasion: How Britain Joined the Common Market* (Thames and Hudson, 1973)

Internet Sites

europa.eu.int/eur-lex/en/com/rpt/2002/act0324en01/1.pdf

Annual report from the Commission on the application of Community law for 2001

europa.eu.int/index_en.htm

Europa, Gateway to the European Union web site

www.europarl.org.uk/index.htm

The UK Office of the European Parliament

CHAPTER SIXTEEN
The Public Sector

INTRODUCTION

When examining the public sector, we need to be aware of a number of different factors. First of all, a definition of the term 'public sector' is required. Thereafter, the actual scope of the public sector needs to be examined. Only then will it be possible to evaluate whether a public sector is needed.

A public sector organisation is one that is geared towards achieving State aims and objectives. Thus there are policies such as nationalisation which bring companies under State control. The provision of education, health and street lighting are also, for the most part, carried out through the State.

The private sector, on the other hand, comprises organisations which are run for the benefit of the owners and/or shareholders. They are not primarily concerned with the aims and objectives of the State. Here we can see organisations such as British Telecom and Severn Trent Water (both of which were privatised), as well as retailers such as Next or Debenhams. Even a corner shop is part of the private sector.

Public Sector

The purpose of this sector is to achieve the aims and objectives of the State. Organisations in this sector are run for the benefit of the public as a whole.

Private Sector

This sector comprises organisations which are run for the benefit of the owners and/or shareholders.

There is a simple test to ascertain whether an organisation belongs to the public sector or the private sector. It is known as the *cui bono* test. It asks 'who benefits from the organisation?' Private sector organisations are run for the benefit of the owners and shareholders. Public sector organisations are run for the benefit of the public. Thus, in a capitalist economy, profits are of great importance to the private sector, whilst quality of service delivery is important in the public sector. While such a distinction appears quite clear cut, the reality is somewhat different. For example, some public sector services, such as refuse collection, are carried out by private sector organisations. In the city of Leicester, a private company (Biffa) collects the refuse on behalf of the council. The private sector is increasing its role in the public sector. Examples include housing, health and education.

This blurring of the public–private divide was brought about in the 1980s by the Thatcher Government. Focusing upon local government, the idea of the State as a 'provider' of services was replaced by being an 'enabler' of service provision. So, rather than providing the actual services, local government had to create a climate to enable other organisations to provide the services on behalf of the local authority. The theory was that the private sector could provide the services more effectively, more efficiently, and far more cheaply than the public sector. It was all part of the Thatcherite scheme to 'roll back the frontiers of the State' – in effect, to reduce the role of the State and State provision of services. By following the application of this ideology, we are left with the question of whether we need the public sector.

Do we need the Public Sector?
The case for retaining the Public Sector

In arguing a case for the retention of the public sector, it is important to note that it does not mean that the private sector should be eliminated. In fact, the public and private sectors often complement each other. In the post-war period, the emphasis was placed upon the idea of a mixed economy. This was a combination of both public and private sectors. Thus there was a public sector National Health Service (NHS) as well as alternative private sector provision. People had the choice as to which they preferred to use. Much of the process of nationalisation in the 1940s and 1950s was implemented not to destroy the private sector, but rather 'to take control of the commanding heights of the economy' as well as to modernise industry in the post-war period. Only the government, through taxation, had the resources to modernise the British economy. The actual extent of nationalisation was quite significant, as can be seen in Table 16.1.

One of the objectives of the public sector is the concept of uniformity of service provision. The idea is to ensure that all members of the public have similar degrees of access to the services. These services include health care, education, benefits, housing, and refuse collection. This concept is often distorted by critics of the public sector. The most blatant form is to describe such uniform provision as 'trying to make us all the same'. Rather, the aim is to make sure that everyone has similar opportunities. If an individual has the wherewithal to provide for themselves (e.g. private healthcare or private education) then they may go ahead and do so. The State will not prevent people from using alternatives. After all, the emphasis is upon a mixed economy – and this can apply as much to service provision as to economic development.

Table 16.1 Industries that were nationalised in the immediate post-war period

Bank of England (1946)

Cable and Wireless (1946)

Civil aviation (1946)

Coal (1946)

Electricity (1947)

Iron and steel (1949)

Gas (1948)

Railways (1947)

Road haulage (1947)

However, there are some services that can only be provided by the State. These are sometimes referred to as social or collective goods. An example of such a good or service would be street lighting. Everyone uses street lighting and pays for it via taxation – specifically their council tax. However, if the private sector were to provide this service what would happen if people refused to pay? How can a private organisation compel everyone to pay for the service? There may be those people who do not want street lighting. The pollution that is caused – and this is not just the light pollution – is so great that street lighting is not justified. Yet these people cannot be prevented from using or benefiting from the street lighting either. Such people are known as free riders. As the label suggests, they would benefit from the private service provision without contributing towards the costs. Thus, the easiest way is for the State to provide this service and have the service paid for via taxation. Other examples of these public goods include pollution control and defence.

One of the problems is that the private sector works on the profit motive. It does not matter what service is being provided, the private sector is motivated by profits. If there is no profit to be made, it is most unlikely that private sector organisations will attempt to provide the service. Thus, even when private sector organisations are involved in service delivery, they are making a profit. This applies to the full range of services from collecting refuse to running schools. While companies such as Biffa and SITA (a French company) have been commended on their service delivery, such experiences are not uniform. In fact, schools in London which have been run by private sector organisations have had some horrendous experiences. Some companies have tried to pull out of contracts for commercial reasons, at a cost of millions of pounds to the council and the Department for Education and Skills.

There are some goods and services which are described as merit goods. These are goods and services such as libraries. A lack of such provision would be considered as detrimental to a community. However, the problem here is that such goods are most unlikely to run at a profit. This is where the State comes in, as private organisations tend not to be willing to support such loss-making ventures – again, we see the profit motive coming to the fore. Such merit goods enhance the quality of life and ought to be provided regardless of cost. The only way to fund such goods is through direct taxation. Everyone then has the opportunity to use and benefit from such goods if they wish to do so.

A final example of the problems that can arise with a dominant private sector and a public sector that is under-financed and acting as a provider of last resort can be seen in the USA. In particular, the health sector in the USA highlights the need for an effective and well-resourced public sector. The system in the USA is based around private health insurance. If you can afford private health care then it is considered to be a fantastic system. The problem is that health insurance costs, on average, over $5000 per year. Such insurance will refund around 90% of the costs of health care. However, around 40 million Americans do not have health insurance. For these people health care becomes prohibitively expensive. The least well off may qualify for the state funded Medicaid scheme. But the rules to qualify for such support vary between the different states of the USA, and are getting tougher. The advice for millions of Americans is 'don't get ill'.

In summary, there is a different ethos between the public and private sectors. The private sector works on the profit motive while the public sector places a far greater emphasis upon service delivery. These two approaches can work in tandem, and can complement each other. However, the importance of the public sector is in making sure that everyone has access to a similar degree of service. This is funded through taxation.

The case against retaining the Public Sector

The case against retaining a public sector is largely ideologically based, and in particular the ideology of the New Right. In the 1980s, Margaret Thatcher spoke of "rolling back the frontiers of the State". The reason for such an approach was that the public sector was seen as inefficient and that it distorted the market. It was claimed that any competition in the market was distorted when the State participated. The State had boundless resources, and could overspend with only little comeback. Private organisations did not enjoy such lack of restraint when it came to spending. In fact such overspending is likely to lead to bankruptcy in the private sector. Yet for the State, if there was a problem, money could be thrown at it. This was expensive for tax payers, often extremely inefficient, and did not always solve the problem.

In contrast, the private sector was seen as being efficient, innovative and entrepreneurial. It would find solutions to problems rather than throwing money at them. The private sector was also competitive. Such competition would benefit the customer or consumer. This would be seen most obviously through cheaper prices and better services. If there was a lack of competition, as a result of a State monopoly, there would be no incentive to develop and innovate. This lack of competition was equated with higher prices, and without necessarily enjoying better service delivery. Where there is competition, the belief is that services will improve and that prices will fall. All of this will benefit the consumer or the client. Such competitiveness is most evident in the private sector. Even where there is competition between public sector provision and private sector provision, assuming there is a level playing field, the competitiveness of the private sector will win through.

This perspective of State control through the public sector was also considered to impinge upon an individual's freedom. The new right approach argues that people should be free to do whatever they want. Any involvement by the State reduces such freedom. Thus high taxes undermine competitiveness and innovation. State provision undermines competition, while excessive State bureaucracy hampers the formation of new organisations. Removing the nanny State would revitalise the country. People would stop being dependent upon the State. They would learn to look after themselves. There would be economic rejuvenation and everyone would benefit. Such is the ideological perspective of the new right. This approach was adopted whole-heartedly by Margaret Thatcher and was retained by her successors, although not necessarily to the same degree.

The Thatcher Government introduced a number of different policies to reduce the role of the State. The most prominent of these was privatisation. This was where public sector organisations were sold off to private investors. A list of the industries that were privatised is presented in Table 16.2. Thatcher's successors continued with the privatisation programme.

Table 16.2 Range of industries privatised or part-privatised by the Thatcher Government

Associated British Ports (1983)

British Aerospace (1981)

British Airports Authority (1987)

British Airways (1987)

British Gas (1986)

British Steel (1988)

British Telecom (1984)

Britoil (1982)

Electricity distribution (1990)

National Bus Company (1986)

Water Companies (except Scotland) (1989)

Other policies to reduce the role and range of the public sector included: Compulsory Competitive Tendering (CCT); deregulation; and, opting out of local authority control. CCT was a scheme whereby specific aspects of local government and health provision were put out to tender e.g. refuse collection. Local authorities were able to present their own tenders for the various contracts but were not always successful. The contracts are short to medium term, rather than permanent. Deregulation enabled private companies to provide alternatives to public sector provision e.g. bus services. This policy was aimed to breaking up public sector monopolies. Finally, the idea of opting out of local government control focused upon education and housing, among other areas. In education, schools were given the opportunity to opt out of Local Education Authority (LEA) control. In doing so, they received their funding directly from central government rather than via the LEA. In housing, as well as the sale of council houses, tenants were also given the option of choosing their landlord – whether they wished to remain under council control or have a private sector landlord.

The drive to reduce the public sector and the role of the State was epitomised in the vision of Nicholas Ridley (Secretary of State for the Environment 1987-89). At the local government level, he envisaged a residual authority. Local government would be, at best, a provider of last resort. All other services could be sold, tendered or contracted out. If there was to be a role for local government, it would be little more than supervising the contracts. Everything that local government did could be provided by the private sector or the voluntary sector. Such a position could easily be transferred to all tiers of government, so that all that would remain would be a residual state.

The public sector is seen as part of a bloated, inefficient state. It needs to be pared back if not removed. It creates a culture of dependence, and is paid for by the rich through taxation. These people have striven to create their wealth and should be left in a position to spend it as they see fit rather than having the state penalise them for earning so much money and redistributing it to layabouts who cannot be bothered to find work. In striving to achieve social equity, supporters of the public sector simply pour resources into a bottomless pit. Rather than looking for alternatives, they simply demand more money. By eliminating the public sector people will be compelled to do something about their position in society rather than depending upon handouts from the State.

Conclusion

What has become apparent in this chapter is an ideological division over the role of the State in general, and the public sector in particular. Supporters of the public sector highlight the need for a basic provision of services that should be available to everyone, free at the point of use. This can be seen as an important feature of the welfare state – Beveridge's statement in 1944 of care 'from the cradle to the grave'.

The problem has been how to fund this welfare state, and more generally the public sector. Taxation has always been the approach used. Yet, supporters of the new right have argued that the rich – in particular, those who use the private sector – are being charged twice, and one of these occasions is for a service that they do not use. The money from taxation is used to provide universal services for all. However, there are those who feel that they can receive better services by 'going private'. These people pay for the universal provision despite not utilising it.

The Thatcher Governments in the 1980s, and all subsequent British Governments, have been searching for ways in which to reduce the cost of the public sector, if not to reduce its size. The idea has been to introduce private sector attitudes into service delivery. The idea being that competition is good, and that customers and consumers benefit from such competition. Yet in doing this, the whole idea of the public service may be diminished. It is not just through cost cutting, but is most noticeable through the idea of the public sector ethos.

In brief, the idea of the public sector ethos is that services are delivered regardless of circumstances. People working in the public sector are not as well paid as their counterparts in the private sector. This matters little. Those working in the public sector do so because of the satisfaction in delivering services properly. Financial compensation (pay) may even be viewed as a bonus. Such an ethos has been undermined through cost cutting, penny pinching and the denigration of the public sector.

The counter side to this is that the public sector ethos is a rather patronising approach to service delivery. It suggests that those who deliver the services know best, and may actually be unresponsive to any change. Changing managerial attitudes have been important. Public sector managers have come to realise that they do not have a blank chequebook with which to fund service delivery. Therefore we see a need to innovate, and to find other ways in which to deliver public services. This can be seen in the demand from Tony Blair that Britain must modernise the delivery of public sector services. Such a statement appears to assume that the public sector is here to stay. The issue is now moving to the form of public sector provision that is needed in Britain today.

Summary of key points

DEFINITION OF THE PUBLIC SECTOR

❐ An organisation in this sector is geared towards achieving State aims and objectives

❐ Public Sector organisations are run for the benefit of the public

❐ Private Sector organisations are run for the benefit of the owners and/or shareholders

THE CASE FOR RETAINING THE PUBLIC SECTOR

❐ Retaining the public sector does not mean eliminating the private sector. Britain has a mixed economy – a mix of public and private

❐ Some goods and services can only be provided effectively by the State. These are social or collective goods

❐ The private sector operates under the profit motive. If there is no profit to be made, the private sector will not provide these goods and services e.g. merit goods

THE CASE AGAINST RETAINING THE PUBLIC SECTOR

❐ Margaret Thatcher – "rolling back the frontiers of the State"

❐ The public sector is bloated and inefficient

❏ The private sector is far more innovative, efficient and entrepreneurial than the public sector
❏ The use of the public sector impinges upon the freedom of the individual

Further Reading

Chapman, R. (ed.); *Ethics in Public Service* (Edinburgh University Press, 1999)

Gray, C.; "Is high taxation the price of a civilised society?" in Robins, L. and Jones, B. (eds.); *Debates in British Politics Today* (Manchester University Press, 2000)

Greenwood, J., Pyper, R. and Wilson, D.; *New Public Administration in Britain Today* (Routledge, 2002) esp. chp.11

Pratchett, L.; "The new ethics of modern public service" *British Journal of Politics and International Relations* vol. 1, 1999

Pratchett, L. and Wingfield, M.; "The Demise of the Public Sector Ethos" in Pratchett, L. and Wilson, D. (eds.); *Local Democracy and Local Government* (Macmillan, 1996)

Worthington, I. and Britton, C.; *The Business Environment* (Prentice Hall, 2003), fourth edition, esp. chp.10

Internet Sites

www.cabinet-office.gov.uk/regulation/publicsector/index.htm

This is the Cabinet Office web page on the public sector. From here it is possible to access a range of sources of information on the public sector.

www.cms.hhs.gov/medicaid/mover.asp

US Department of Health and Human Services overview of the Medicaid programme.

CHAPTER SEVENTEEN
The Media

INTRODUCTION

The media is an essential part of the British political scene. Its role is considered to be vital in enhancing our democratic system. Yet the term 'media' covers a vast array of areas. Most obviously there is television, radio and newspapers. To this list can be added magazines, books, journals and the internet. Within each of these areas, there are many subsets. For example there is the basic divide in newspapers between broadsheets and tabloids. However, this is now becoming a little blurred with two broadsheets – *The Independent* and *The Times* now printing both broadsheet and tabloid versions. For television viewers, there are the basic five channels from which to choose in the UK, unless you subscribe to satellite, digital or cable providers, where you may get access to hundreds of channels.

The media

This term is used to cover television, radio, newspapers, magazines, books, journals and the internet. The media is used to communicate news, information and opinions to its users.

This chapter is going to focus largely upon the broadcast and newspaper media. In particular, the emphasis is upon the reporting of news events. Having an open and free media enables a potentially wide range of news reports of the same event. Such breadth of reporting would appear to leave much scope for bias. This may actually leave the media open to the accusation of manipulating the news, or reporting events in such a way as to potentially distort them. In the reporting of news there is a divide between reinforcement theory and agenda setting. Each of these approaches will be examined in greater detail later in the chapter, but a brief comment will be made here. Reinforcement theory is where the media reinforce existing opinions. Thus readers or viewers will pick the sources of information that pander to their opinions. Agenda setting, on the other hand, is where the media influences what people think. By concentrating on specific issues or concerns, the media can generate a band wagon effect. Both of these approaches (reinforcement theory and agenda setting) have some credence, but the question remains as to the extent to which the media manipulates events.

Do the media manipulate events?

The media does manipulate events

The suggestion that the media does manipulate events falls neatly into the agenda setting theory. The current perception of agenda setting is more to do with influencing what people think about rather than what people think. Instead of pushing a particular perspective on an issue, it is more to do with raising the issue per se. This could be seen over the issue of weapons of mass destruction in Iraq. The issue was raised and discussed in the media, but it was not as if the media were trying to tell people what to think on the subject.

Yet media ownership, especially in the print media, often leads to biased reporting. Newspaper ownership can be seen in Table 17.1. The owners of particular newspapers have particular issues – or more accurately, aspects of particular issues – which they would like to be raised and addressed. Such an example of this was on the campaign to name of alleged paedophiles in 2000, orchestrated by the *News of the World*. The editor at the time, Rebekah Wade, later became editor of *The Sun*. The *News of the World* printed the names and photographs of alleged paedophiles, claiming that this was in the interests of the public, as the government was not acting to protect the public from paedophiles. A number of people were forced to flee from vigilante groups in Portsmouth, Plymouth and other towns around the country. To make matters worse, some of the alleged names that came into the public domain were inaccurate, or people with the same name were illegally targeted. Thus a number of innocent people were harmed or forced to flee. A huge outcry was generated on the issue of paedophiles but it went out of control very quickly. The *News of the World* eventually backed down on the publication of further lists as a result of the outcry against it – including from its sister paper The Sun.

It is not just on the reporting of such controversial issues that there is media bias. In the reporting of election campaigns there is overt bias in the print media. The broadcast media have an obligation to be even-handed – no such restriction applies to the print media. Thus, after the 1992 General Election, *The Sun* claimed "It was The Sun wot won it". The Sun claimed to have won that election for John Major. Their persistent attacks on the Labour Party, and the Labour leader Neil Kinnock, were claimed to have swung a number of wavering voters back behind the Tories. On polling day, The Sun front page showed a picture of Neil Kinnock in front of a blue light bulb with the statement that if this man became Prime Minister, would the last person to leave the country please turn out the light.

Table 17.1 Newspaper Ownership in Britain

Daily Papers	Owners	Approximate Circulation
Daily Express	Northern and Shell	879 000
Daily Mail	Daily Mail and General Trust	2 323 000
Daily Record	Trinity Mirror	499 000
Daily Star	Northern and Shell	883 000
Daily Telegraph	Hollinger*	873 000
Financial Times	Pearson	417 000
Guardian	Guardian Media Group	363 000
Independent	Independent Newspapers	229 000
Mirror	Trinity Mirror	1 847 000
Sun	News International	3 361 000
Times	News International	611 000
Sunday Papers	**Owners**	**Approximate Circulation**
Independent on Sunday	Independent Newspapers	178 000
Mail on Sunday	Daily Mail and General Trust	2 255 000
News of the World	News International	3 849 000
Observer	Guardian Media Group	417 000
People	Trinity Mirror	1 028 000
Sunday Express	Northern and Shell	885 000
Sunday Mirror	Trinity Mirror	1 566 000
Sunday Telegraph	Hollinger*	678 000
Sunday Times	News International	1 316 000

★ At time of writing, Hollinger were looking at selling their interests in the Daily Telegraph and Sunday Telegraph.

Yet, it is interesting to note just how fickle newspaper support can be. Table 17.2 shows which newspapers supported which party over the last three general elections. The Express newspapers, led by Richard Desmond, have declared recently that they can no longer support Labour and have reverted back to the Conservatives. Rupert Murdoch, owner of *The Sun*, *The Times*, Sky Television, Fox Television, and a host of other interests, appears to be toying with both parties. Both Tony Blair and Michael Howard appear desperate for an endorsement from this Australian media magnate. It is interesting to note that although *The Sun* is listed as supporting the Labour Party in the 2001 and 1997 elections, the reality is, as their headline stated: "The Sun Backs Blair".

Table 17.2 Party Support of Newspapers at General Elections

Newsaper	Party Preference in 2001 (1997, 1992)
Daily Express	Labour (Conservative, Conservative)
Daily Mail	Conservative (Conservative, Conservative)
Daily Star	Labour (Labour, No endorsement)
Daily Telegraph	Conservative (Conservative, Conservative)
Financial Times	Labour (Labour, Labour)
Guardian	Labour (Labour, Labour)
Independent	Labour (Uncommitted, Uncommitted)
Mirror	Labour (Labour, Labour)
Sun	Labour (Labour, Conservative)
Times	Labour (Euro-sceptic, Conservative)

Two other events where the media reporting was considered by many commentators to be over the top were the death of Diana Princess of Wales, and the war in Iraq. In the case of the death of Diana, there was saturation coverage in both the print and broadcast media. It was reported that there was a national outpouring of sympathy. Almost all other news stories were pushed to the sidelines. In the case of the BBC, all non-Diana programmes were removed from the schedules of both terrestrial television channels. Those who were uninterested in the subject — or who were heartily sick of the coverage — had few options available to them.

The reporting on the war in Iraq was also at saturation level. This war, more than any other, was broadcast into the living rooms of almost every house in Britain. Twenty four hour television news is available in the UK, including BBC News 24 and CNN. These television channels were filled with the war on Iraq. Added to this, reporters were 'embedded' into units, and were able to report from the frontline. However, this led to the 'fog of war' appearing in the broadcasts. The port of Um Qasr was reported to have been taken by British troops on a number of occasions before it actually fell. Many such stories were reported live without being fully substantiated. The same applied to the print media coverage as well. The daily press briefings from the US Headquarters were generally uninformative, with hostile questions not being permitted. Broadcasters who questioned the US role in Iraq or who questioned the actions of American or British troops, such as the Arab satellite broadcaster Al-Jazeera, were barred from the press briefings.

A final subject to raise on the media manipulating events is the European Union. A number of newspapers appear fundamentally opposed to British membership of the EU. Some daily papers, notably *The Sun, The Daily Mail, The Express,* and *The Daily Telegraph* have consistently attacked the EU, to the extent of printing stories with little more than a veneer of truth to them. There is no balance in their reporting, nor is there any obligation to provide such balance. Consequently, the vast majority of those who read these newspapers have little idea of any benefits that Britain gains through membership of the EU. Should Tony Blair ever hold a referendum on the Euro or the EU constitution, he is going to have to battle overwhelming odds in the face of the rabidly euro-phobic press.

The agenda setting role of the media is thus quite obvious. Particular newspapers – or more accurately their owners – have a specific line to push on any given issue, be it Europe, Iraq, immigration or whatever. This constant stream of bias moulds public opinion. The broadcast media is also similar. The venues of interviews give particular credence to one side of a story over another. The protestor or trade union official is interviewed in front of a noisy backdrop, while the business person or government minister tends to be interviewed in a quiet office or lounge. One side portrays noise, the other is calm. The status quo must not be upset.

The media does not manipulate events

The whole idea that the media manipulates events is something of a distortion. The agenda setting perspective needs to be questioned. Instead, the media provides what can be described as reinforcement theory. The media reinforces their readers or viewers opinions. Rather than setting the agenda, the media responds to it. If readers do not like what they read in a newspaper or magazine, they will change. If they do not like what is being reported on the television or radio news, they can change channel. Overt bias which is not in line with the broad perspective of the reader or viewer will be scorned.

An example of the reinforcement theory can be seen with the reporters embedded into military units during the Iraq war. There was no way in which these reporters were able to falsify reports – there were a number of inaccuracies but, as noted earlier, much of this could be attributed to the 'fog of war'. Rather, the reporting was more sympathetic to the general public's support for the British military, if not for the operation they were carrying out. On top of this, with the vast number of international broadcasters reporting on the war, by accessing a range of different information sources via the internet, anyone could see the extent of bias from particular sources. Thus, for example, the propaganda emanating from Fox News was unquestioning in the role of US troops and their actions in Iraq. The Al-Jazeera network, on the other hand, questioned the actions of US and British troops all of the time. This was even more frequent after US troops 'mistakenly' bombed the Al-Jazeera office in Iraq.

An area in which the broadcast media is bound to be impartial is over reporting of elections – local, regional, general or European. There is an obligation on broadcasters to have balanced coverage of any news events. Thus during an election campaign, the Conservatives and Labour will have similar amounts of air time, with the Liberal Democrats having slightly less. In Scotland and Wales, the Scottish Nationalist Party and Plaid Cymru will both be given comparable amounts of regional air time to the three larger parties. Other smaller parties get far less coverage, dependent upon their success in previous elections. Specific issues could be highlighted that may favour one party or discriminate against another, but the media watchdogs such as the ITC (Independent Television Commission) and the BSC (British Standards Commission) monitor television programmes for such bias and sometimes attempt to curtail any imbalances.

A final aspect to note is that it is not necessarily the media which attempt to manipulate events but rather the politicians themselves. All major parties use media managers, or spin doctors. It is their job to ensure that not only the correct stories are broadcast or published, but also that the correct perspective is also presented. Alastair Campbell has been the most prominent of all spin doctors, even surpassing the fame of Bernard Ingham (spin doctor for Margaret Thatcher). Alistair Campbell was credited with utilising the phrase "the People's Princess" after the death of Diana – a phrase used frequently by Tony Blair at the time. Campbell has also been prominent over the Hutton Inquiry and frequently attacked the BBC for inaccurate or biased reporting of events. He even turned up during a Channel 4 news broadcast and demanded to be interviewed – much to the surprise of Jon Snow.

However, these spin doctors sometimes get things wrong. After the terrorist attack on the twin towers on 11 September, 2001, Jo Moore (then-spin doctor for Stephen Byers in the Department of Transport, Local Government and the Regions) e-mailed colleagues saying that it would be a good day to bury bad news. Five months later, allegations were made against her that she had made a similar suggestion at the time of the funeral of Princess Margaret (the Queen's sister). While such events are often viewed as an opportune moment to publish damaging news, to actually encourage such actions is considered reprehensible. Jo Moore survived the original error thanks to the support of her minister, Stephen Byers. The second, which she did not actually do, led to her resignation. So spin doctors are not always successful in manipulating the news, except in so far as they become the news!

It is not just the government that attempts to spin the news. Private organisations also employ media consultants (a fancy term for spin doctors) to protect their own interests. McDonalds, for example, have had to fight allegations of beef in burgers being sold in India, accusations of the levels of salt and fat in their food being far too high, and even a threatened ban on advertising. While their marketing division will be prominent in any such response, their spin doctors needed to respond with speed.

With the restrictions on reporting for the broadcast media, and attempts by the government – or in fact any organisation – to place a positive perspective on any news affecting them, it is highly unlikely that the media can manipulate events to further their own agenda. Individual media publishers/broadcasters will present the news in a manner that their audience wishes. To do otherwise would lose sales with a knock on effect of lost advertising and lost revenue. The challenge for the media is to present the news by seeing through the spin.

Conclusion

The media has changed markedly over recent years. From newspapers and magazines, television and radio, it is now being enhanced by the internet. This form of media may eventually replace all others. The list of newspaper websites below (see internet sites) is far from exhaustive, and their archive sections are phenomenal. We can watch television or listen to the radio on our computers. E-journals may even replace paper – although this is highly unlikely. Yet this is what the future may hold, and some of it is already here.

The knock on effect of this change in the media would be evident in a drop in newspaper circulations or in viewing/listening figures for the broadcast media. Surprisingly, in almost every area, the figures are dropping. Whether this is due to technology, or a disinterest in the news, is difficult to say.

In an attempt to keep viewers, listeners and readers, the media appears to be dropping down to the lowest common denominator. This is the idea of dumbing down. Rather than presenting the news with critical analysis, many papers now focus on gossip: the lives of celebrities – who is sleeping with/leaving/marrying/divorcing whom. It is not just the newspapers and magazines that are doing this, but also the broadcasters. Viewers can interact with news programmes. Thus, for example, on the BBC's Breakfast programme, viewers' e-mails are read out. It could be suggested that this is part of the reinforcement theory, whereby the media report on what the viewers want to know. These e-mails may be a step too far.

As for the question of whether or not the media manipulates events, there is no clear cut answer. For every example where the media may be seen to manipulate the news, there will be a counter example. As the media develops further, with greater choice of programmes and greater use of the internet, who knows how the media will respond in its endless chase for viewers or readers.

What this chapter has demonstrated is that there is no straight forward answer to the question of the media manipulating events. At best, there is indicative evidence to support both sides of the case. The evidence is not absolute. As each case is presented, like the media, we need to be critical of what is said.

Summary of key points

DEFINITION OF THE MEDIA

- ❏ A term used to cover a number of forms of communication of information to the public
- ❏ These include television, radio, newspapers, journals and the internet

THE CASE FOR THE MEDIA MANIPULATING EVENTS

- ❏ This is often portrayed as agenda setting
- ❏ The media highlight stories, or particular aspects of them
- ❏ The objective is to raise a particular issue. The slant on the story will present the position
- ❏ The enthusiasm with which top politicians appear to pander to the whims of newspaper owners

THE CASE AGAINST THE MEDIA MANIPULATING EVENTS

- ❏ This is often presented as reinforcement theory
- ❏ The media report on the stories that the public want to see
- ❏ The media responds to the agenda of the public (or possibly that of the government)
- ❏ Use of spin doctors, not just by the government but also by almost every organisation, to present a story in a particular light

Further Reading

Greenslade, R.; *Press Gang: How newspapers make profits from propaganda* (Macmillan, 2003)

Kuhn, R.; "The Media and Politics" in Dunleavy, P., Gamble, A., Heffernan, R, and Peele, G. (eds.); *Developments in British Politics* 7 (Palgrave, 2003)

Negrine, R. (ed.); *Television and the Press Since 1945* (Manchester University Press, 1998)

Stokes, J. and Reading, A. (eds.); *The Media in Britain: Current Debates and Developments* (Macmillan, 1999)

Internet sites

www.aljazeera.com/

Home page of the Al-Jazeera Network (English edition)

www.bbc.co.uk

The BBC home page

www.cnn.com/

Home page of CNN

www.dailymail.co.uk

Home page of the Daily Mail

www.foxnews.com

Home page of the Fox News channel

www.guardian.co.uk/

The Guardian web page

www.independent.co.uk/

The Independent home page

www.itn.co.uk/

ITN (Independent Television News) Homepage

www.mirror.co.uk

The Mirror homepage

www.sky.com/skynews/home/

Home page of Sky news

www.telegraph.co.uk/

Home page of the Daily Telegraph

www.thesun.co.uk

Home page of The Sun

CHAPTER EIGHTEEN

The Environment

INTRODUCTION

Environmental issues have been around for many years. However, it was only really in the 1960s and 1970s did they begin to gain any major public support. A significant turning point in British Politics was the 1989 elections to the European Parliament, where the Green Party gained 15% of the vote – although due to the vagaries of the Simple Plurality electoral system, they gained no representation. It was really from that election that the major political parties started to take environmental concerns more seriously.

The Environment

An overarching term to cover the physical resources that exist. These include the land, sea and air. Environmentalists are concerned with the protection of these physical resources, as well as the life forms that exist within them.

Yet, when examining 'the environment', it is often unclear as to what should be included. Some environmental concerns are quite obvious: pollution, acid rain, preserving fishing stocks or the traditional countryside. To this can be added concerns over nuclear waste, oil leaks, foot and mouth, BSE, GM crops, pesticides, chemicals in food (such as preservatives and E numbers), animal welfare, hunting and other blood sports. The list seems to go on and on. A list of some environmental disasters is presented in table 18.1, and it is by no means exhaustive.

As well as all of these disasters, there are the ongoing ones such as sewage; the hole in the ozone layer over Antarctica; continued global warming; the destruction of rainforests in, among other countries, Brazil and Indonesia; the extinction of many species of animal, including the dodo (in Mauritius) and the moa (in New Zealand) – neither of which can be described as recent events, and the near-extinction of others such as the Siberian tiger. All of these are environmental disasters.

Table 18.1 Environmental disasters

1957	Windscale, Cumbria	Nuclear reactor fire
1966	Aberfan, Wales	Coal slag heap slid and buried a school
1967	Torrey Canyon	Oil spill off the Cornwall coast
1979	Three Mile Island, USA	Partial nuclear reactor meltdown
1984	Bhopal, India	Chemical leak in Union Carbide factory
1986	Chernobyl, former USSR	Nuclear leak/meltdown
1989	Camelford, Cornwall	Polluted water released into mains supply
1989	Exxon Valdez	Oil spill off Alaska
1980s/90s	BSE (Mad Cow Disease)	Outbreak in British cattle, linked to CJD in 1996
1993	Braer	Oil spill off the Shetland Islands
1996	Sea Empress	Oil spill off the South Wales coast
1999	Erika	Oil spill off the Brittany coast
2000/1	BSE	Outbreak in continental Europe
2001	Foot and Mouth outbreak	Traced to a farm in Northumberland
2002	Prestige	Oil spill off the Spanish coast
2003	BSE	First reported case in USA

The environment is of great importance to everyone. Yet its protection, or preservation, is often overlooked. Much of this is to do with our economic system – capitalism. The underlying premise of capitalism is profit-maximisation. Care and preservation of the environment costs a great deal of money. Thus there is little incentive to protect it. Even the idea of sustainable development – where you replace the economic resources that you consume – struggles to fit in with capitalism. It would be feasible to present a case suggesting that capitalism and sustainable development are diametrically opposed.

Some countries appear far more concerned with protecting the environment than others. The US administration of George W. Bush would probably top the list of developed countries that place the environment low on their list of priorities. Yet, within Europe, the country that appears to be the least concerned with the environment is Britain. In fact in the 1980s, Britain earned the label 'the Dirty Man of Europe' – and this was from the environmental movement in Britain. In 1990, Chris Rose published *The Dirty Man of Europe: The Great British Pollution Scandal*. This highlighted many of the environmental problems in Britain, and the lack of will power to do anything to redress the situation. Approaches such as 'dilute and disperse' were used, where pollution was pumped into the sea or the air, or hidden in landfill. In each case, the pollution would be diluted by the air, water or land, and would then disperse – in theory harmlessly. Even as counter-evidence massed up, Britain persisted with a 'dilute and disperse' approach.

Table 18.2 Reasons for Britain earning the label 'the Dirty Man of Europe' in the 1980s

Export of pollution	The North Sea currents and airstreams propelled British pollution elsewhere
A uniquely bad polluter	Britain was the biggest importer of radioactive waste, and was one of the largest producers of CFCs and sulphur dioxide
Procrastination	Persistently calling for further research rather than action e.g. on acid rain
Treatment of symptoms not causes	Use of 'dilute and disperse' approaches in areas such as landfill, oil pollution, and sewage
'Perfidious Albion'	Distorting information to delay action or avoid responsibility
Toleration of public squalor	Failed to invest in modern litter bins and allowed public transport to deteriorate
Impeding of the law	Evaded EU directives
Abuse of science	Wanted to test the environment after the damage is done despite the indications of ecological change

Derived from *Rose, C.; The Dirty Man of Europe: The Great British Pollution Scandal* (Simon and Schuster, 1991) pp. 296-297

This list in Table 18.2 demonstrates the apparent lack of care or interest in environmental well being. Despite many of the problems in the list being redressed, the problem has been that the label 'the dirty man of Europe' has stuck. In fact, in some areas, the list has lengthened. Britain is associated with pollution and lack of care for the environment, and is seen to be enthusiastic about GM crops but also oblivious to fears over BSE, foot and mouth, and so forth. One of the more recent proposals (in 2003) was to pump carbon dioxide waste from power stations under the North Sea. Such a move would enable Britain to meet pollution targets for 2050. The consequences of such an approach were fiercely debated. In 2004, there was the suggestion of shooting Britain's nuclear waste into the sun. This was one of fourteen different proposals to get rid of this pollution. With these types of schemes being proposed, the question to ask is whether or not the label 'the dirty man of Europe' is still justified.

Is Britain still 'the dirty man of Europe'?

Britain is still 'the dirty man of Europe'

One of the major reasons why Britain earned, and has kept the label, is to do with ideology. In the 1980s, Britain moved from a mixed economy, with a major role for the state, to a more market-led economy. The role of the government was greatly reduced (see Chapter Sixteen for more information). It became a 'hands-off' approach to most aspects of the economy and the environment. Thatcher's Government saw no need for the state to interfere on environmental issues – the market would resolve any problems. Whenever bodies such as the EU made proposals on environmental issues, the British Government (of either political persuasion) would block them or water down the proposals to such an extent that they became meaningless. Hanley (1998, p.57) provides the example of the Bathing Water Directive of 1976:

> [This] imposed high standards on designated bathing waters. In an attempt to limit the potential cost of implementing the Directive, the Government designated only the twenty-seven waters which already met the standards laid down, implying in the process that the beaches of many seaside resorts were not bathing waters.

The outcry from a range of environmental groups, as well as tourist bodies, eventually compelled the Government to adjust its position and invest in cleaning up the British seaside.

The Conservative Governments of the 1980s and 1990s emphasised deregulation of public sector monopolies as well as a policy of privatisation. An emphasis was placed upon the right of the individual to choose. This idea of 'choice' was considered a fundamental freedom. In the transport sector, deregulation and privatisation, along with the idea of 'choice', saw policies being developed with the emphasis upon road-building.

> Road-building was used as the main policy tool to tackle traffic congestion, with the justification coming from some of the central tenets of the new right; those of individual freedom (narrowly defined as freedom to drive a car at virtually any point in space or time); and economic competitiveness, translated as the need for efficient road links for business… The policy emphasis was therefore on mobility rather than accessibility, with the benefits biased strongly towards those able to travel by private car. (Vigar, 2002, p.2)

Thus, despite some EU partners wanting strong, tight regulations, what Britain wanted was loose regulation of the environment – flexibility was key. Whereas the British wanted general broad brush guidelines, with room for manoeuvre, other EU members desired a far more proactive approach to environmental regulation. Such an approach flew in the face of both the Thatcher and Major Governments with regard to the role of the state, as already noted above.

Part of the problem for Britain with the label 'dirty man of Europe' is the importance given to the post holder. Table 18.3 lists all of the Secretaries of State for the Environment. Few of the post-holders could be considered high on the 'Green' ladder: the most prominent would be Chris Patten, with Michael Meacher (who was only a Minister of State under Margaret Beckett) probably the most 'Green'. The Department of the Environment was created in 1970, with the merger of the Ministry of Housing and Local Government and the Ministry of Transport. This was the first cabinet-level department of its kind. Transport became a separate department between 1976 and 1997, when it was reabsorbed into a new super department. For most of its existence, the Department of the Environment has had other departments mixed in with it. This has seen the importance of the environment diminish. In the late 1980s and early 1990s, for example, with local government under the remit of the department anything to do with the environment was at best secondary to the Poll Tax!

An important reason as to why Britain earned the label 'the dirty man of Europe' has to do with pressure group politics. The environmental lobby in Britain appears to be far better mobilised than our EU counterparts. The sheer volume of groups is phenomenal. The Friends of the Earth web pages list hundreds of different groups under a variety of subject areas, ranging from biodiversity and habitats to climate change, from energy to food and trade (see *www.foe.co.uk/pubsinfo/infosyst/other_services.html* for the full list of organisations cited).

Although there are a large number of pressure groups in the environmental sector (see Chapter Nine for more information on pressure groups), not all of them have access to the decision makers – be it at local, regional, national or the European level. However, the volume of groups and the ability to get their voices heard has meant that these groups have been able to apply pressure on the decision makers. Success is by no means guaranteed – to name two high profile protests: the Newbury by-pass was built, and Manchester Airport had a second runway built. Such developments, despite all of the protests, encourage the belief that Britain does not care about the environment.

Table 18.3 Secretaries of State for the Environment

Department	Secretary of State
Housing and Local Government/Environment	Peter Walker (1970-2)
Environment	Geoffrey Rippon (1972-4)
Environment	Anthony Crosland (1974-6)
Environment	Peter Shore (1976-9)
Environment	Michael Heseltine (1979-83)
Environment	Tom King (1983)
Environment	Patrick Jenkin (1983-5)
Environment	Kenneth Baker (1985-6)
Environment	Nicholas Ridley (1986-9)
Environment	Chris Patten (1989-90)
Environment	Michael Heseltine (1990-2)
Environment	Michael Howard (1992-3)
Environment	John Gummer (1993-7)
Environment, Transport and Regions	John Prescott (1997- 2001)
Environment, Food and Rural Affairs	Margaret Beckett (2001-)

Although people seem better informed about environmental concerns, they appear unwilling to do much to improve things. In the example of recycling, of the 15 member states (prior to the 2004 enlargement), Britain was ranked thirteenth, with only 12.4% of waste being recycled. This is compared to 64% in Austria, 52% in Belgium and 47% in the Netherlands. The position on renewable energy is almost as bad. Of the 25 member states in the EU, Britain is ranked twentieth, with only Poland, Belgium Hungary, Estonia and Malta ranked worse.

In some respects, Britain seems to pride itself on the label 'dirty man of Europe'. There is actually a huge source of revenue to be made from pollution. Successive British Governments have assisted in a range of decontamination schemes, where other states effectively export their waste to Britain. A recent example was the so-called 'ghost ships', four of which were exported from the James River, Virginia USA to Hartlepool in the Northeast of England. These ships were to be dismantled in dry dock and the hazardous waste disposed of in landfill sites. In total, there were to be thirteen ships being broken down in Hartlepool, despite local protest.

To the local population, the scheme was presented as being of huge economic benefit to the area. Around 200 jobs would be created, with the deal itself worth over £10 million. Yet the environmental cost was played down. The asbestos and other carcinogens would be disposed of in a landfill site – the re-emergence of the policy of 'dilute and disperse'. These poisons may simply filter into the ground, causing massive contamination.

To make the situation even worse, some of the ships were not considered fit to cross the Atlantic Ocean – and none of them would be fit to make a return journey should they be forced to leave Britain. Wherever they sailed, a huge slick of pollution would be left in their wake. They were not permitted to travel through the English Channel, and the Scottish Executive and the Irish Government demanded they not enter their respective fishing waters. With this type of pollution importing going on, Britain does still appear to be 'the dirty man of Europe'.

Britain is no longer 'the dirty man of Europe'

The idea that Britain is 'the dirty man of Europe' is something of a myth. The concept was used to challenge politicians and officials into amending Britain's environmental policies. It was a form of scare mongering used by well organised pressure groups to distort the extent of environmental concerns. In the 1980s, when this label came to the fore, the loose regulatory approach adopted by the Government of the day had some success in addressing a number of environmental concerns. The formation of the Industrial Air Pollution Inspectorate in 1982 to monitor air pollution was such an example, along with a number of other inspectorates on waste, water quality and radioactive substances (Garner 1996). Yet the idea that if the government is not actively legislating or regulating on environmental issues then there is a problem is fundamentally flawed. Rather than coercing organisations into protecting the environment, a more gentle hands-off approach actually encourages many organisations to participate in environmentally-friendly schemes.

In fact, when drawing in the European Union, Britain has a good track record of implementing EU legislation on the environment. Successive British Governments may have complained very loudly about over-regulation from Brussels, but once the legislation is passed, Britain implements the legislation. As Garner (1996, p. 123) notes: "the record of implementation and enforcement is not as bad as one might expect given the unfortunate publicity Britain often receives". This is in contrast to some of our EU partners who demonstrate an acute awareness of environmental issues, but are not so efficient at implementation and enforcement. On environmental issues, Britain has a good record on implementation, even though it is not always evident - Table 15.2 highlights the implementation records on all issues, not just the environment, where Britain sank from seventh to fourteenth in 2001.

With the enlargement of the EU, many of the new members who joined in 2004 have less than exemplary environmental records. There are ongoing tales of US agribusiness relocating to countries such as Poland. As environmental regulations are less well enforced than in countries such as Britain, these companies appear to have a free hand to pollute through their factory farming. Although there is localised protest, little appears to be happening in response to the alleged polluting.

Environmentalism is so far behind in the East European accession states that EU structural funds are being used to build water treatment plants. All of these new member states are playing catch up with the current members. Part of the problem, which is no longer so prevalent in Britain, is a lack of knowledge and information on environmental issues. For example, only one of the new members of the EU from Eastern Europe gained representation for the Green grouping in the European Parliament – and that was Latvia, with one of their MEPs.

Although Britain seems to get a bad press over environmental issues, much of it undermines the positive work achieved. For example, in 1994, the Conservative Government took up the issue of sustainable development, proposing a Strategy for Sustainable Development. This led to the formation of the Sustainable Development Commission, which first met in 2000. The most recent report from the Sustainable Development Commission (in April 2004), chaired by Sir Jonathan Porritt, was subtitled: "Shows Promise But Must Try Harder". Britain is making steps, and in some respects may be leading the way in addressing environmental issues in Europe, but there is no room for complacency. In reducing carbon dioxide emissions, the British Government has played a key role in developing an EU position. Caps will be in place on the amount of emissions from each site across the EU, and the EU Emissions Trading Scheme will commence in January 2005. This is all part of the plan to cut EU greenhouse emissions by the 8% target set at Kyoto. Britain is well on track to surpass its target, but countries such as Italy and Austria have hardly developed a feasible plan. Britain developed its' own Emissions Trading Scheme in 2002, and as a result will not join the EU version until 2007. According to the Department of the Environment, Food and Rural Affairs, in the first two years of operating, there was a reduction in emissions equivalent to almost 10 million tonnes of carbon dioxide.

In many of the global schemes to protect the environment, Britain has also played a key role. The Rio 'Earth Summit' (June 1992) which led to both Agenda 21 and the Convention on Climate Change, and the Kyoto Summit (December 1997) which strengthened the Convention on Climate Change, both saw active British participation. Not only did Britain play an active role, especially at Kyoto where John Prescott was most forthright in expressing his views, but since then the British Government has been persistent in attempting to achieve the targets set by these Summits, as well as persuading other governments to do the same.

Agenda 21, as outlined at the Rio Summit, focuses upon sustainable development. The key aspects of Agenda 21 are detailed in Table 18.4. It is interesting to note that Agenda 21 does not focus simply upon the 'traditional' aspects of the environment and conservation, but also upon the political, social and economic aspects as well. All tiers of government, from local to supra-national, have to plan sustainable development strategies. The expectation was, and has been realised, that a series of partnerships would develop between governments and non-governmental organisations. For example, at the local government level we can see partnerships between the public sector and the private sector on refuse collection and recycling.

As noted above, the Kyoto Protocol strengthened the Convention on Climate Change. More stringent targets were set to reduce greenhouse gas emissions by 2012. While most EU members (including Britain) were enthusiastic about the Kyoto Protocol, others were less so – most notably the USA, but also countries that claimed to be to the forefront in 'Green Politics' such as Australia, Canada and New Zealand. Rather than having some degree of flexibility between developed and less developed states, these four countries along with Japan demanded uniform targets across the world. Ultimately the US Government, under the Presidency of George W. Bush, refused to ratify the Kyoto Protocol. Evidently the high consumption, high polluting lifestyle of the average American was non-negotiable.

With both the Rio Summit and the Kyoto Protocol, we see Britain to the forefront in protecting the environment at the global level. Closer to home, many other steps have been taken – particularly post-1997. Not only was the Sustainable Development Commission established in 2000 (as mentioned earlier in this chapter), but also the UK Environment Agency which was created in 1997. The Environment Agency, like the Sustainable Development

Commission, is a quango (see Chapter Eight for the debate on quangos). By creating a quango, the government hoped to take the party politics out of the environment debate.

Table 18.4 Agenda 21

Social and economic dimensions	Highlights the relationship between environmental concerns and problems of poverty, health, trade, debt and population
Conservation	Focuses on the management of physical resources (sea, air, land) to promote sustainable development
Strengthening the role of different groups	Highlights the need to draw in different groups who have active roles to play, including: women, indigenous populations, local authorities, voluntary organisations, trades unions, business, industry, the agricultural sector and science
Implementation	Examines how governments and non governmental organisations can enable such policies to be implemented

Developed from *Connelly, J. and Smith G.; Politics and the Environment: from theory to practice* (2003) p. 240

The Environment Agency has a wide remit, as can be seen in Table 18.5. It covers a number of different areas, issuing Position Statements. Each Position Statement highlights key issues, the Agency's role and their proposed solutions, along with a full background briefing on the particular subject area. The Environment Agency works closely with Government Departments and other non-governmental organisations.

A final point to note about Britain being perceived as 'the dirty man of Europe' is that Britain takes global environmental concerns very seriously indeed. The case in Hartlepool of the 'Ghost Fleet' highlighted British concern for the environment. It is far better for such a fleet of ships to be dismantled in a safe and secure environment, as was to be done in Hartlepool, rather than being either left to rot or be cut up on an open beach somewhere. There have been cases of heavily polluted ships (with asbestos and other cancer-causing pollutants) being dismantled with oxyacetylene torches in both India and Turkey, and the workers in these cases had no access to any protective clothing. Thus, it is far better for Britain – and other countries which have safe facilities – to destroy such vessels.

Table 18.5 Subjects on which the Environment Agency has issued Position Statements

Air Quality

Brownfield Land Redevelopment

Environmental Taxation

Managing Hazardous Waste

Regeneration

Responding to Climate Change

Sustainable Construction

Waste Incineration

Water Framework Directive

Derived from the Environment Agency website at
www.environment-agency.gov.uk/aboutus/512398/289428/?version=1&lang=_e

Conclusion

The accusation that Britain is 'the dirty man of Europe' is still controversial. The label itself was engineered because of an apparent lack of concern for environmental issues – and it was seen as a way in which to compel the government to be more active in protecting the environment. In reality, it may have been more to do with Britain as a 'reluctant European' in the 1980s rather than environmental performance (Lowe and Ward, 1998, p.288). Britain's track record on the environment can be described as uneven. The British Government has been seen to be promoting and protecting the environment at major conferences such as Rio and Kyoto. However, the actions are not so forthright. The Rio Summit, for example, "placed particular emphasis on the damage road-based transport was doing to the biosphere" (Vigar, 2002, p6). Britain was quite enthusiastic about such a move, yet ten years later road building continues apace: more roads, more cars, more pollution, and more destruction of the environment. It is little consolation that Britain is not the worst offender. To call Britain 'the dirty man of Europe' is unfair and inaccurate. Britain tends to adopt a pragmatic approach to environmental issues, just like most EU members.

Summary of key points

DEFINITION OF THE ENVIRONMENT

❏ A general term to cover the physical resources. These include land, sea and air

❏ Environmentalism is about protecting these resources, as well as the life forms that exist within them

❏ Is sustainable development compatible with capitalism?

THE CASE FOR BRITAIN BEING 'THE DIRTY MAN OF EUROPE'

❏ In the past there has been limited government involvement in protecting the environment. A 'hands off' approach has been utilised

❏ The environment has never been seen as a priority for policy makers

❏ Pressure groups have been key in raising environmental issues and mobilising public opinion

❏ In areas such as recycling and renewable energy, Britain has performed very badly when compared to other EU members

THE CASE AGAINST BRITAIN BEING 'THE DIRTY MAN OF EUROPE'

❏ The label has always been something of a myth, used by pressure groups for scare mongering

❏ The 'hands off' approach to the environment has been successful in getting British businesses to be more environmentally aware, without using heavy handed regulation

❏ Compared to other EU members, particularly the new East Europeans, Britain has a very good track record on environmental concerns

❏ Britain has been to the forefront at both the Rio Earth Summit and at the Kyoto Summit, and in persuading other states to participate fully (except the USA)

Further Reading

Carter, N.; *The Politics of the Environment: Ideas, Activism, Policy* (Cambridge University Press, 2001)

Connelly, J. and Smith G.; *Politics and the Environment: from theory to practice* (Routledge, 2003) 2nd edition

Garner, R.; *Environmental Politics* (Prentice Hall, 1996)

Hanley, N.; "Britain and the European policy process" in Lowe, P. and Ward, S. (eds.); *British Environmental Policy and Europe: Politics and Policy in Transition* (Routledge, 1998)

Humphrey, M.; "Environmental Policy" in Dunleavy, P., Gamble, A., Heffernan, R. and Peele, G. (eds.); *Developments in British Politics* 7 (Palgrave, 2003)

Lowe, P. and Ward, S.; "Lessons and Prospects: The prospects for the UK environment in Europe" in Lowe, P. and Ward, S. (eds.); *British Environmental Policy and Europe: Politics and Policy in Transition* (Routledge, 1998)

Lowe, P. and Ward, S. (eds.); *British Environmental Policy and Europe: Politics and Policy in Transition* (Routledge, 1998)

McCormick, J.; "Environmental Policy" in Cram, L., Dinan, D. and Nugent, N. (eds.); *Developments in the European Union* (Macmillan, 1999)

Rose, C.; *The Dirty Man of Europe: The Great British Pollution Scandal* (Simon and Schuster, 1990)

Vigar, G.; *The Politics of Mobility: Transport, the environment and public policy* (Spon Press, 2002)

Internet sources

www.defra.gov.uk

Homepage of the Department of the Environment, Food and Rural Affairs

www.environment-agency.gov.uk

Homepage of the UK Environment Agency

www.foe.co.uk

Homepage of Friends of the Earth

www.sd-commission.gov.uk

The Sustainable Development Commission homepage

www.un.org/esa/sustdev/agenda21.htm

Agenda 21 website

www.unfcc.org

The United Nations homepage for the Convention on Climate Change

CHAPTER NINETEEN
Gender

INTRODUCTION

It was not until 1918 that women received the vote in Britain, and a further ten years until parity with male voting rights was achieved. At that time, it was felt (at least in male circles) that the women's rights movement had achieved its aims. This is anything but true. There is still a high degree of inequality, not just in Britain but globally. "Women's lives are regulated and conditioned, for example, by the legal status of wives, by government policies on childcare, by the allocation of welfare benefits, by labour laws and the sexual division of labour, and by laws on rape, abortion, sexual harassment" (Freedman, 2001, pp. 28-29). Thus there is still a need for women's rights to be addressed properly. The problem is that we live in a male-dominated society, where women's rights appear secondary.

Feminism

There are a number of different approaches towards feminism. At one level, it is a movement that seeks to raise women's social status. There are then divisions as to how such an aim can be achieved. These include separatism, where men cannot be accepted a allies in the cause, through to a more liberal approach which seeks reform through equal rights legislation.

Glass ceiling

This is where career paths of women are blocked before they can reach the top of an organisation. The top positions may appear achievable but their attainment is blocked by men.

The 'ideology' that promotes and defends the rights of women is feminism. It is concerned with women's inferior position in society and how to address this position. However, as with many ideologies, there is no single branch of feminism. There are a number of different approaches to feminism, including political, economic, environmental and epistemological. (For further information on these various approaches see the Feminist Theory Website at Virginia Tech University at *www.cddc.vt.edu/feminism/index.html*.) A key aim of feminism is to raise the social status of women. The issue is how this can be done. The different approaches have diverse ideas as to how such an aim can be achieved. Some are reformist – using legislation – while others are more radical, if not revolutionary, refusing to have any dealings with men or accepting support from men.

Another key issue is the role of the state in promoting and defending the rights of women. Radical feminists would argue that this is counter-productive as men control the legislative process. Any concessions made to women would still be to the benefit of men more than women. Reformists would be more enthusiastic about the role of the state. Legislation can compel organisations to address gender issues. In fact, in terms of equality of social status, women have attained better positions in countries where the state has been active in work-family arrangements (van Doorne-Huiskes, 1999, pp.93-4).

Yet while there may be all of this activity from the state in promoting the rights of women, a major issue still remains. While there appears to be equality of opportunity for women, there is the suggestion that a glass ceiling still exists. The career paths of women seem to be blocked before they reach the top of an organisation. Despite all of the legislation to promote equal rights, the upper echelons of most organisations are male dominated. Women are unable to break through this glass ceiling.

Is there still a glass ceiling?
The case against there still being a glass ceiling

The idea that the glass ceiling still exists is flawed. Government legislation has been in place now for over thirty years to protect women's rights. The list of Acts of Parliaments and EU legislation is quite comprehensive, as can be seen in Table 19.1. The Sex Discrimination Act (1975) established the Equal Opportunities Commission in the following year. The role of this commission is to investigate breaches of the Sex Discrimination Act and the Equal Pay Acts. Ultimately, the role of the Equal Opportunities Commission is to eliminate discrimination in Britain. The idea is to fight discrimination in the work place. This is not just sex discrimination (with which this chapter is dealing) but also discrimination by ethnicity, disability, age, etc.

Table 19.1 Legislation to promote equality

British legislation

Equal Pay Act (1970)

Sex Discrimination Act (1975)

Equal Pay Act (1983)

Employment Rights Act (1996)

National Child Care Strategy (1998)

New Deal 1998

Sex Discrimination (Election Candidates) Act (2002)

Equal Pay Questionnaire (2003)

EU Legislation

Treaty of Rome (1957) Article 119

Equal Pay Directive (1975)

Equal Treatment Directive (1976)

Social Charter, part of the Maastricht Treaty agreement (1992) accepted into British law in 1997

Amendments (2002) to the Equal Treatment Directive to be implemented by 2005

What has been evident over the last quarter of a century is the huge social change that has taken place in Britain. Some of this has been a result of the legislation in Table 19.1. Yet it is also a consequence of both the liberal policies of the 1960s and 1970s as well as the neo-liberal policies of the Thatcher era. As noted in Chapter Sixteen, the belief was that anybody could do anything. There was an equality of opportunity. Gender was no barrier, as could be seen with Britain's first woman Prime Minister. In 1997, there were more women elected to Parliament than ever before, while in the Welsh Assembly in the 2004 election, 50% of the representatives were women. As a result of many of these changes, most of which were not through legislation, the role of women has improved. This is often best seen through educational attainment. The female pass rates at both GCSEs and 'A' levels (grade A★ to C) has far surpassed that of males for a number of years (not just overall but in every subject area), and when examining the number of university undergraduates women are surpassing men again. There are still more male graduates in Britain, but this data is skewed due to the number of older women who were unable to go to university. Overall, these changes are feeding into the economy and society. More and more women are now in the work place and attaining better posts.

Legislation may have assisted in this, but, from a neo-liberal perspective, it is not necessary.

In 1994, the Wainwright Trust sponsored a report into family-friendly and equal opportunities policies entitled "Parents at Work". This report highlighted the steps taken by both public sector and private sector organisations in promoting and developing such policies. The report was quite enthusiastic about the steps taken to that time. The Wainwright Trust has been actively promoting equal opportunities in the workplace since the mid-1980s, in gender, ethnicity and disability.

The Labour Government since 1997 has taken even more steps to promote fairness and equality. A Ministry of Women was established in 1997 as part of the Cabinet Office. Currently there are two Ministers for Women (Tessa Jowell Secretary of State for Culture, Media and Sport, and Meg Munn who is based in the Department of Trade and Industry. They are supported by the Women and Equality Unit. By 2001, over a third of all appointments to public bodies were women. After the Welsh Assembly elections of 2004, both the Assembly and the Executive were dominated by women (see Table 19.2).

Table 19.2 Female Representation in British Politics

House of Commons (1992)	9.2%
House of Commons (1997)	18.2%
House of Commons (2001)	17.9%
House of Commons (2005)	19.8%
House of Lords (2003)	16.4%
Senior Civil Service (2002)	23.3%
Welsh Assembly (1999)	40.0%
Welsh Assembly (2003)	50.0%
Welsh Executive (1999)	66.7%
Welsh Executive (2003)	55.6%
Scottish Parliament (1999)	37.0%
Scottish Parliament (2003)	39.5%
British Members of the European Parliament (1999)	24.0%
British Members of the European Parliament (2004)	24.4%

In the policy realm, child care support and other issues that are considered to be part of the role of women have been addressed with the New Deal legislation of 1998. This is an ongoing process – it is not as if the job has been completed. The New Deal focuses upon employment opportunities for everyone, and is broken down into specific subsets e.g. lone parents, 18–24 year olds, etc.

In March 2004, a luncheon was held at Buckingham Palace for around 180 women to celebrate female achievement. Those invited included a number of prominent women in Britain today such as Cherie Booth (lawyer), Hilary Armstrong (Government Chief Whip), Margaret Beckett (Government Minister), Charlotte Church (singer), Lorraine Heggessey (Controller of BBC1), Nicola Horlock (City financier), Mary Quant (fashion designer), J. K. Rowling (authoress) and Lady Thatcher (first woman Prime Minister in Britain). This may have been a celebration of "girl power", but it also highlighted the success of women today. Looking at these successful women, it is possible to say that the glass ceiling has been broken.

The case for there still being a glass ceiling

The idea that the glass ceiling has been broken is false. There are still barriers that exist which prevent women achieving their full potential, and these barriers are controlled by men. We live in a patriarchal society. The term means dominance by the father, or more generally, men dominating women in society. With such male dominance, the glass ceiling remains intact.

Women who are considered 'economically active' tend to have two jobs. The first may be their paid job, while the second is that of domestic work and is unpaid. Domestic work remains primarily a woman's responsibility (van Doorne-Huiskes, 1999, p. 97). In fact the role of most men around the house is at best negligible. The vast majority of men do not participate in domestic chores or play a far reduced role in childcare. According to the Equal Opportunities Commission, women spend three times as much time as men on child care (*www.eoc.org.uk/cseng/abouteoc.asp#_Equal_Chances?*). This provides a huge handicap for any woman with career aspirations.

The number of women in top posts is still very small. Huge headlines were printed in October 2003 when Dame Brenda Hale became the first female law lord. She took up the post in January 2004. The fact of the matter is that there are very few women in top posts in almost every profession. Women now comprise around 45% of the British work force. Most of the jobs held by women are concentrated in Public Administration, Education and Health (around 40% of women's employment). After these, the next most prominent sector of employment is in services such as hotels and catering. Yet when looking at the management levels, just over 10% of management posts are held by women – even in sectors which are dominated by female employment.

Yet it is not just in employment that there are problems. Rates of pay – even when doing the same job – still differ. In 2003, the gap in pay on the basis of gender was at its smallest ever. This is 34 years after the Equal Pay Act was passed, and there is still a difference in payment. On average, women in full time employment earn £396 per week, while men earn £525. However, such a statistic distorts some of the argument. The Equal Pay Act is about equal pay for equal work rather than about gender equality per se. So, when examining specific sectors, there is about a 25% pay gap in weekly pay in the education sector, almost 30% in health and social work, and about 45% in banking and insurance. (For full details on the pay gap go to the National Statistics Office web page at *www.statistics.gov.uk* or the Equal Opportunities Commission web page at *www.eoc.org.uk*).

Where attempts have been made to address gender equality issues, and ultimately breaking the glass ceiling, it has been through legislation. The European Union has been prominent in fighting for gender equality (see Table 19.1 for a list of EU regulations). As Meehan and Collins (1999, p. 136) have noted: "the existence of EU policies and institutions helped British women to circumvent a domestic political climate that was, until recently, inhospitable to intervention in respect of women's interests". The idea of little or no state intervention, as espoused by the Thatcher and Major Governments of the 1980s and 1990s, clearly had no positive effect on the position of women. See Chapter Sixteen for more detail on the role of the State. Thus it was the European Union that became vitally important on all social issues. If anything, the Thatcher Government tried to encourage women to adopt a more traditional role of housewife and child minder.

The current Labour Government has attempted to improve the position of women. In 2002, the Sex Discrimination (Election Candidates) Act was passed. This provided for women-only short lists for political parties when selecting electoral candidates, as well as training for the selection committees. This is not positive discrimination as it is sometimes portrayed in the right wing media where it is often seen as an evil. Rather, it is a pro-active attempt to encourage women to stand as electoral candidates, and to encourage selection committees to consider female candidates. With so few women standing as candidates, it is hardly surprising that politics seems largely irrelevant and out of touch to so many people.

Conclusion

The idea of gender equality in Britain has still not been achieved. Legislation has helped to protect the interests of women but the glass ceiling still exists. There are some things that legislation cannot improve, and it may well be the case that the revolutionary feminists are right. A case in point was the comments made by the UK Independence Party MEP, Godfrey Bloom, in July 2004. Bloom had attempted to join a committee on women's rights in the European Parliament, where he said he wished to defend men's rights. Although thwarted, Bloom's publicly stated position on women's rights caused what could be described as consternation among MEPs and women's rights campaigners. He believes that women who get pregnant should resign from their jobs, and that women's issues are more to do with cleaning behind the fridge properly. Bloom's defence was that such a position was a fact of life and that he should know because he was a business man. As long as such a Neanderthal position is maintained by one of our elected representatives then there is little chance of breaking the glass ceiling through legislation.

Thus what women's rights campaigners are fighting is a mind set. No amount of legislation can change what people think (see Chapter Two on Political Culture). To change such a mind set requires education. For example, when children play doctors and nurses, why must the girls be the nurses? In 21st century Britain, you would think that gender issues (and all other inequality issues) would have been addressed. For over thirty years, legislation has been in place to promote and defend gender equality. Yet even now, some of those same battles are still being fought. The glass ceiling is one of the more obvious symbols of gender inequality.

Summary of key points

DEFINITION

◻ Feminism is a movement that seeks to raise women's social status

◻ There are a range of different approaches from the more radical and revolutionary through to the more liberal

◻ The Glass Ceiling is where the career paths of women are blocked before they can attain the top positions

THE CASE AGAINST THERE STILL BEING A GLASS CEILING

◻ Much legislation has been passed to protect women's rights at both national and European levels

◻ Women are achieving success at all levels of society. The successes tend not to be publicised

◻ It is not the role of the State to promote and protect women. From a neo-liberal perspective, everyone should look after themselves regardless of their gender

THE CASE FOR THERE STILL BEING A GLASS CEILING

❑ We live in a Patriarchal Society

❑ The legislation that has been passed may have improved the position of women but there is still inequality e.g. gender pay gap (Equal Pay legislation was passed in 1970!)

❑ Attempts to improve the lot of women tend to be portrayed as Positive Discrimination, or 'political-correctness gone mad'

Reading list

Baker, S. and van Doorne-Huiskes, A. (eds.); *Women and Public Policy: The shifting boundaries between the public and private spheres* (Ashgate, 1999)

Davidson, M. and Cooper, C.; *Shattering the Glass Ceiling: the woman manager* (Paul Chapman Publishing, 1992)

Freedman, J.; *Feminism* (Open University Press, 2001)

Grant, M.; "Feminism: political success or economic disaster?" in Robins, L. and Jones, B. (eds.); *Debates in British Politics Today* (Manchester University Press, 2000)

Heywood, A.; *Political Ideologies: An Introduction* (Palgrave, 2003) 3rd edition

Lister, R.; *Citizenship: Feminist Perspectives* (Palgrave, 2003) 2nd edition

Meehan, E. and Collins, E.; "European Policies and Women's Rights in the United Kingdom" in Baker, S. and van Doorne-Huiskes, A. (eds.); *Women and Public Policy: The shifting boundaries between the public and private spheres* (Ashgate, 1999)

Randall, V. and Waylen, G. (eds.); *Gender, Politics and the State* (Routledge, 1998)

Squires, J.; "Politics Beyond Boundaries: A Feminist Perspective" in Leftwich, A. (ed.); *What is Politics?* (Polity Press, 2004)

van Doorne-Huiskes, A.; "Work-Family Arrangements: the Role of the State versus the Role of the Private Sector" in Baker, S. and van Doorne-Huiskes, A. (eds.); *Women and Public Policy: The shifting boundaries between the public and private spheres* (Ashgate, 1999)

Watkins, S., Rueda, M. and Rodriquez, M.; *Introducing Feminism* (Icon Books, 1999)

Internet sites

www.cabinet-office.gov.uk/wnc/index.htm

Home page of the Women's National Commission

www.eoc.org.uk

Equal Opportunities Commission home page

www.fawcettsociety.org.uk

Home page of the Fawcett Society, a group campaigning for equality between men and women

www.newdeal.gov.uk

Government web page for the New Deal, a strategy to get people back to work

www.radicalphilosophy.com/

Home page of the Radical Philosophy journal, which is a journal of socialist and feminist philosophy

www.statistics.gov.uk/

Home page of the National Statistics Office

www.wainwright.trust.btinternet.co.uk/

Home page of the Wainwright Trust which is an equal opportunities development trust

www.womenandequalityunit.gov.uk/

Home page of the Women and Equality Unit (WEU) which works to develop policies relating to gender equality

www.womens-unit.gov.uk

The Women's Unit home page

CHAPTER TWENTY

Conclusion

INTRODUCTION

During the writing of this book, there have been a number of significant events that have changed the face of British politics – Peter Mandelson was appointed an EU commissioner, Dame Brenda Hale was appointed to the Law Lords, a war in Iraq has been fought (and is continuing to be fought, despite George W. Bush claiming that the war was won in May 2003), Ken Livingston has rejoined the Labour Party, and the Swedes voted against joining the Euro. To some people, these changes may seem minor, or even inconsequential. But they have all had an impact on the political landscape. Yet despite these and other events, the more things change, the more they stay the same. We have a government with a large Parliamentary majority that seems almost unstoppable. There is an Opposition party that seems ineffective and is being challenged by others to be seen as the viable opposition to Tony Blair. There is a central government that appears willing to walk over all other tiers of government, as well as public opinion. It is no wonder that more and more people seem unenthused about participating in politics.

Yet in this system of British politics, its key underpinning is democracy. As noted in Chapter One, we live in a liberal democracy. The democracy aspect is the idea of people ruling (*demos* and *kratos*). The liberal aspect focuses upon various freedoms, many of which we take for granted. These were detailed in Table 1.1. Many of them are protected through the Human Rights Act, which was examined in Chapter Four. The question asked about the Human Rights Act is whether or not it goes far enough in protecting our rights. It is possible for the legislation to be suspended, as has already occurred. And in August 2004, the Shadow Home Secretary, David Davis, announced that a future Conservative Government would repeal the Human Rights Act as it had spawned a litigious society. Davis was condemned by many human rights activists and others within the legal profession as trying to undermine our basic rights. The amount of litigation in British courts has increased, but not directly as a consequence of the Human Rights Act.

So to protect our liberal freedoms, perhaps we do need a Bill of Rights built into the British constitution – a piece of legislation that can not be repealed by a future government on a whim. In our democracy, we take our liberal freedoms for granted whereas they actually need protecting.

Another aspect of British democracy that has been highlighted throughout this book is the right to participate. The most obvious example of this participation is voting. After all, Britain has a representative liberal democracy. Yet levels of participation in voting appear to be falling. Only 59% of those eligible to vote actually did so in the general election. Levels of turnout at local, devolved and European elections in 2004 were even lower. This highlights a number of problems in our democracy.

The first of these is the extent of centralisation – not just to Westminster, but to the executive and even the prime minister. With the emphasis so much upon Tony Blair and his cabinet, other tiers of government simply do not get a look in. Even the local election results get transposed on to Westminster, with the infamous line: "Had this been a General Election, Parliament would look like..." Thus many people are giving up on other tiers of government – even the new devolved bodies in Scotland, Wales and Northern Ireland. Whether having directly elected devolved bodies in England will make a difference to this centralisation remains to be seen.

Another question mark remains over the use of the Simple Plurality electoral system for our Parliamentary elections. There has been a suggestion that a change in the electoral system will stimulate turnout. The evidence to support such a position is a little sketchy. The elections to the devolved bodies and the European Parliament use different electoral systems. Their turnouts have not improved. This could be to do with the extent of centralisation, as noted above. However, other countries that have changed their electoral systems for their parliamentary elections have seen something of a backlash against the new system. A case in point here is New Zealand, where a large section of public opinion wants to revert back to using Simple Plurality.

Where participation has increased in British politics is in the realm of pressure groups and protests. Well over 1.5 million people marched in London to protest about the war in Iraq in February 2003. Never before had British public opinion been mobilised in such a fashion. The Countryside Alliance has never had such numbers in support of its position, nor the Poll Tax protestors in 1990. The disappointing thing was that the Government ignored the public. Despite the protests, the war went ahead. Tony Blair claimed to be listening to the people (the idea of democracy) but that he had to make the final decision and the people had to trust him. The weapons of mass destruction have yet to be found and will never be as they did not exist. The trust that Blair asked to be placed in him has been lost. This was clearly obvious in the Leicester South by-election in 2004, where a safe Labour seat was lost to the Liberal Democrats and George Galloway's Respect Party candidate performed remarkably well. This suggests that it is worthwhile participating in politics. You can not expect to be successful all of the time. Pressure group campaigners know that they must try, try and try again. It is a matter of mobilising public support.

Yet there are still aspects of our British democracy that appear undemocratic. There are issues of accountability and responsibility. Our elected representatives are accountable and responsible to the public. It is possible to vote them out of office at an election. The problem is that there are aspects of our political system that are unelected, and are sometimes seen to be unaccountable.

Within government, an area that is sometimes portrayed as being undemocratic is quangos. These non-elected bodies are portrayed as having a democratic deficit – a lack of democracy. If they are unelected, how can they be held to account? Arguably, this is done indirectly, via the parent department and government minister. How can, for example, the Secretary of State for Education and Skills be held responsible for the actions of a school board of governors? Some schools that have opted out of Local Education Authority control have had to co-opt members of the public on to their boards just to be quorate. Why should the Secretary of State be held to blame for the actions of such a board? It is not always feasible for ministers to be held responsible for the actions or inactions of their civil servants, even less so their quangos. It becomes very difficult to find the accountability here.

Beyond government, the role of pressure groups and the media may also appear undemocratic. There are some well organised pressure groups, such as those campaigning against speed cameras, which are anything but representative of public opinion. Their claim that speed cameras infringe our rights is crass. This suggests a right to break the law. Speed cameras may be a lucrative source of revenue but they do appear to be a necessary part of the campaign against drivers who speed. Some groups have fire bombed speed cameras, thrown paint over them, and in some cases chopped them down. Can such illegal actions be considered acceptable within our liberal democracy? We do have the right to protest, and to voice our concerns (freedom of speech), but only within the bounds of the law. The claim that speed cameras infringe our rights is dubious but the mindless vandalism of the speed cameras can not be condoned.

The media is another aspect of our society that appears undemocratic. Newspapers often claim to be speaking on behalf of the people but the main objective of their owners is to make money. An obvious example of an issue that has been distorted by poor reporting in the media is the European Union.

Some newspapers are rabidly opposed to anything to do with the EU. These newspapers – in particular *The Sun* and *The Daily Mail* – take every opportunity to denigrate the actions of the EU. The idea that the EU could actually be good for Britain, or that signing up to the European constitution or even the Euro would benefit Britain, is not even considered. These newspapers are able to spout their propaganda without any real accountability. The Press Complaints Commission seems unprepared to raise the issue of balance. Should Britain hold a referendum on either the European Constitution, or the Euro, the bile that will emanate from the Euro-phobic press will be phenomenal. The idea of balanced, even-handed reporting will be non-existent in these newspapers. There is no counter-balance in these newspapers. The most enthusiastic about the EU is probably *The Guardian*. But when examining the levels of readership (see Table 17.1), there is no contest. The Euro-phobic press will claim that they are merely reporting what their readers want to hear – pandering to their readers whims. The idea of presenting both sides of the argument in a clear manner, and then letting the readers make up their own minds does not seem worthy of consideration.

The problem here is that within our liberal democracy, one of the key features is an open press. The government should not be able to control or manipulate the media. The media should be (largely) free to report what they feel the public wants to hear or needs to know, within the bounds of the law. Thus it could be viewed as essential to democracy that we have this media reporting news and events from a perspective that is not in line with the government of the day. The concern is when the media appear to get too powerful – as could arguably be seen with both Tony Blair and Michael Howard pandering to the whims of Rupert Murdoch. In such a circumstance, how can the media be constrained without undermining any of the democratic tenets of British politics and society?

This private ownership of the media raises another important aspect of our British democracy – the role of the public sector. Chapter Sixteen raised the question as to whether the public sector was still needed. A case was put which suggested that everything done by the public sector could be carried out by other organisations, such as the private sector or the voluntary sector. Yet the role of the State is a key feature of our democracy. The consensus of opinion is that the State has an obligation to protect everyone within its geographical boundaries. However, the issue is over the extent of the protection. Is it merely an army to protect our borders, or a police force and judiciary to maintain law and order? What about the provision of education or health? If there is no State provision, what happens to those who cannot afford to utilise the private option? It could be argued that the State's 'protection' of its people should include housing, health, education, pensions, water and other utilities, the environment, transportation, as well as the police, army and judiciary. The ideological divide over the role of the State is huge. During the 1980s and 1990s, the dominant ideology in Britain – that of the New Right – had as a key aim the 'rolling back of the frontiers of the State'. Many aspects of State provision were privatised or were removed from the direct ambit of the government. When the Labour Party won the 1997 General Election, many people expected the new government to reverse the policies of the Thatcher and Major Governments. Those who said it would never happen were tarred as cynics. "Things can only get better" was the theme. Things have got better in many instances, but the rolling back of Thatcherism has not been included. The cynics were right. The role of the State within our democracy is still important, but it has been reduced.

In conclusion, we do still live in a liberal democracy, although to some people it may not always feel so. The various chapters of this book have had, as their underpinning, this issue of democracy in Britain. Be it the modernisation of Parliament, enthusiastic participation in the EU, or the gradual politicisation of the civil service, they are all linked to democracy. Many people using this text will have read some of the chapters in isolation. There are times when we need to take a more holistic approach. The chapters are all inter-linked. Sometimes it may not appear obvious, but the issues examined within each chapter do impact upon the others. The important point is that we must not take everything for granted. If people stop participating in our democracy, how can they hold the decision makers to account?

INDEX

Essential Topics in
MODERN BRITISH
POLITICS
and
GOVERNMENT